"If you live long enou..., ... crushing disappointment that life in a broken world brings. Jennie Pollock understands disappointment and longing, and lovingly shows us where lasting peace can be found when life is not what you expected it to be."

COURTNEY REISSIG, Author, *Teach Me to Feel*

"This is a timely message for our generation, filled with the wisdom that comes from living something rather than merely talking about it. Jennie's meditations on contentment will strengthen anyone wrestling with an 'if only' in their Christian life."

ANDREW WILSON, Teaching Pastor, King's Church London

"This book is for anyone who has ever wondered why God is withholding the very thing their heart desires. I found myself nodding in agreement on every page. Biblical, insightful and immensely helpful."

VANEETHA RISNER, Author, *The Scars That Have Shaped Me*

"This is a beautiful, brave book. Jennie is not afraid to probe our doubts and fears. But in so doing, she shares deep truth which not only consoles but becomes the bedrock of life. This book is to be read, treasured and given away!"

WENDY VIRGO, Speaker; Author

"*If Only* invites the reader to take an honest look at the God who loves us, even when things aren't going the way we dreamed. Practical, Scripture-filled and a wonderful gift to the church."

CATHERINE PARKS, Author, *Real*

"This is going to become one of my go-to books. I loved it. Jennie writes with such reality and warmth, and the truths will sparkle from the pages even in the midst of dark times."

CAROLYN ASH, Former Ministry Wives Conference Organiser, The Proclamation Trust

"In *If Only*, Jennie Pollock allows her readers to be honest and then invites us to learn how true and joyful contentment is possible in Christ. This book is an encouragement to refocus our gaze on our Saviour."

CAROLYN LACEY, Author, *Extraordinary Hospitality (For Ordinary People)*

"Refreshingly honest. I found a richness and challenge in Jennie's writing, and came away pondering much in my own life. I heartily recommend this book."

CLAIRE MUSTERS, Author, *Taking Off the Mask*

"Are you missing something in your life? This book is for you. Jennie Pollock acts as a friend and guide, sharing her hard-earned wisdom in finding contentment, through heart-rending stories and the rich wisdom of the Bible."

AMY BOUCHER PYE, Author; Speaker and Retreat Leader

"A warm, compassionate and encouraging book for anyone struggling to find contentment in the face of painful realities."

JO SWINNEY, Author; Speaker

"If God were an ocean, we would have barely dipped our feet at the shore. In *If Only*, Jennie invites us to come deeper into the water, and see if he isn't the ultimate source of contentment we need."

SHERIDAN VOYSEY, Broadcaster; Author, *Resurrection Year*

"Here's a book that draws you in and helps you feel like you're enjoying a chat over a coffee with a friend. Thoughtful, evocative and warmly practical."

ANTONY BILLINGTON, Senior Pastor, Beacon Church; Theology Advisor, London Institute for Contemporary Christianity

JENNIE POLLOCK

IF
ONLY

Finding joyful contentment in the
face of lack and longing

If Only
© Jennie Pollock 2020

Published by:
The Good Book Company

thegoodbook.com | thegoodbook.co.uk
thegoodbook.com.au | thegoodbook.co.nz | thegoodbook.co.in

Unless indicated, all Scripture references are taken from the Holy Bible, New International Version. Copyright © 2011 Biblica, Inc.™ Used by permission.

ISBN: 9781784984489 | Printed in the UK

Design by André Parker

CONTENTS

INTRODUCTION

I'm not sure when I started wanting to get married. It was just something I expected would happen naturally. My parents met and married young, and I always assumed that by my mid-twenties I would be married with at least a couple of kids. I know that long before I hit 30 I was already longing for it.

As I write these words, I'm 47 and still single.

I spent years praying for a husband—sometimes diligently, sometimes desperately, sometimes despondently. But the desire was always there—the hope that *this* wedding, *this* party, *this* event would be the place where we would meet; the extra alertness when meeting new people; the tendency to check the left hand of any vaguely passable or interesting man... and the disappointment when, yet again, it wasn't to be.

MIND THE GAP

If you're reading this, I'm guessing that you're living with an "if only" too: an area of life where things aren't working, a circumstance you wish were different, a lack or longing that you're reminded of daily. Whether it's a big thing or a little thing, there's a gap between expectation and reality that you can no longer avoid.

I'm also starting from the premise that you're a Christian. That means that by definition you have at some point said, "God, I trust you. I've tried it my way and it didn't work. Please forgive me, on the basis of Jesus' death and resurrection. I acknowledge that you know what is best for me, and I choose to submit to your will." In fact, to be a Christian is to continue saying that to God, day by day. Yet it can be hard to keep going when life doesn't pan out the way we expected—and it's certainly hard to keep going *joyfully*.

As I have listened to many people's stories over the last few years, and as I reflect on my own, it seems to me that there is a "contentment gap", that sits between our expectation of what the Christian life should be like and our experience of it. This gap may have started as a tiny crack, a fissure between the overflowing joy of our love for Christ and that one little circumstance that still nagged on the edges of our consciousness. Over time, the crack widened until it formed a crevice, a canyon, a yawning chasm, filled with our doubts, fears and questions about this God who was supposed to give us "fullness of joy" (Psalm 16 v 11, ESV). Just as water can, with time and persistence, carve channels out of solid rock, so our unmet expectations or unaddressed desires can erode our joy— the spouse who we no longer "click" with, the job that doesn't fulfil us, or the budget that constantly constricts us. From the bottom of the valley we can see the sun, but we can't feel its warmth, and we wish we could find a way to the surface to enjoy it again.

Or maybe the canyon was created overnight. When COVID-19 swept the world in 2020 many people lost jobs, homes and security—not to mention loved ones. Maybe the earth was ripped from beneath your feet in a catastrophe like that and you found yourself, dazed and confused, in a landscape that was barely recognisable.

How do we climb out of this canyon? Is it even possible?

THE SECRET

One man who had experienced life in the canyon was the apostle Paul. When he wrote his letter to the church in Philippi, he was being held captive in Rome because of his Christian faith—in a house rather than a jail, but still in chains and under guard (see Acts 28 v 16, Philippians 1 v 12-14). He was unable to work or to travel around preaching, as he had loved to do, and he had rivals on the outside who were now taking advantage of his imprisonment (Philippians 1 v 15-18). Not to mention that becoming a Christian in the first place had meant a significant loss of face, loss of reputation, loss of status, in fact, loss of everything Paul had been working for his entire life. He had given it all up for Jesus... and look where it had got him! If anyone had the right to feel he'd got a raw deal from God, Paul certainly did.

And yet his letter to the Philippians is just bubbling over with joy and delight. He had "learned the secret of being content in any and every situation" (Philippians 4 v 12).

When Paul talks about the secret of being content, he doesn't mean finding a peaceful life. He's not picturing the kind of contentment exhibited by a well-fed cat, curled up by the fire purring. Or by an old farmer, leaning on a gate, gazing across fields of waving wheat and healthy herds. Or by a baby burbling happily in her cot, unaware of the storms of life raging outside her window. These are wonderful visions of peace and security, moments of calm in a difficult and stressful world, but we know that they'll only ever be short-lived.

The contentment that Paul speaks of and exhibits is much more lively and active than that. It didn't cause him to sit back and let life wash over him. No, it motivated him more than ever to speak and write and sing about Jesus and his wonderful, life-changing power. It drove him to live well in the midst of his circumstances and encourage others to do the same.

Contentment isn't a denial of our problems, a lack of ambition or an end of hope. It is not about looking on the bright side or finding what the title of one book memorably calls the "splashes of joy in the cesspools of life". ("I'm single, but I get sole control of the remote"/"We're childless, but we get to go on holiday in term time"/"I'm bedridden, but hey, I never have to do laundry!") Even when our "bright sides" are altruistic—

"My lack of a family gives me the freedom to minister to the needy in my community"—they will eventually leave us burned out or wanting more if they are solely our human efforts to distract ourselves from our pain, or make the best of a bad job.

Christian contentment is much more hopeful than this. It is the fruit of the joyous discovery that whatever our circumstances, Jesus is better by far. It is boundless riches (Ephesians 3 v 8), overflowing thankfulness (Colossians 2 v 7), "exceeding great joy" (Matthew 2 v 10, KJV).

I know that sounds like an impossible dream right now. You can't imagine how it could ever be true, not for you, not really. I hope, in the following pages, to convince you that it can, and to point you to the hand- and footholds on the wall of the canyon with which you can climb back up to find it. While I'll be drawing on my experience of singleness, the way out is essentially the same whatever our "if only" is.

Contentment doesn't usually appear overnight. Paul said it was something to be learned; the 17th-century puritan writer Jeremiah Burroughs described it as something we can and should become "well skilled in" (*The Rare Jewel of Christian Contentment*, p 19). Before we turn to some practical tips for how to train our hearts and minds in this skill, though, we need to start by addressing the big, core questions that our hearts start to ask when we can't see God's hand at work. These are questions that seem to underpin the writings of many of those who have fought the battle of discontentment and won:

Is God good—can I trust him that his way is best?

Is he enough—can he really meet all my needs as he claims?

Is he worth it—is living his way a sacrifice worth making?

I know you know the "right" answers to those questions, the Sunday school answers, the answers we sing in church services and know in our heads to be true. But what about our hearts? That can be a whole different matter—and that is the matter that matters.

CONTENTMENT FOR YOUR EVERYDAY

This isn't just a book for the disappointed. Reading it isn't about resigning yourself to not getting the one big thing you really want and working out how to live with the "if onlys". It's about finding joyful contentment on a regular Tuesday, when there's nothing really wrong, but you suspect there must be more to life than this; or when Christmas and family holidays just aren't the fairy tale that Instagram says they should be.

Jesus said he came that we might have life in all its fullness. Is that really achievable? Here and now? On this grey Tuesday/wet Wednesday/muggy Thursday? Yes, it is. Ironically, it might be easier for those of us living with broken dreams to take hold of that promise, because we've got no one but God to look to for our strength, hope and joy. But the offer is there for everyone who puts their trust in Jesus. Come and see.

Chapter 1

WHO BEFORE WHAT

We are a culture that loves to take action. Glossy magazines and click-bait websites make their living from this impulse, offering endless lists of five ways to improve your sex life, six tricks to reduce stress instantly, or three simple steps to a healthy lifestyle. Any time a problem pops up, we want to know what to do about it.

It's all too easy for us to approach contentment in the same way. The day-to-day pressures on us are real and urgent. We're consumed by the things we're missing in life, whether that's a nicer home, a fulfilling job or a longed-for baby. And so our problem-solving mindset goes to work on finding a way to get what we lack—we save more diligently, scour more job adverts, or push for an appointment with a different fertility specialist.

None of these things are wrong in themselves. But they won't deliver the lasting contentment we think they will. At best they will be temporary or partial fixes, before we start to notice another lack that we need to fix. Nor is contentment achieved by mastering a set of helpful spiritual practices or healthy Christian habits. True contentment is always found in a "who", not a "what". It's about God—our heavenly Father, our risen Saviour and our indwelling Spirit. That was the secret that the apostle Paul said he had learned, in his letter to the church in Philippi (see Philippians 4 v 11-13). He was focused on God, not his circumstances—the "who", not the "what".

Of course, that's a truth which is easy to write, but not so easy to live. Sometimes we long for things so deeply that it's hard to imagine that a world where we don't have that desire fulfilled or issue resolved could ever really be the life in all its fullness that Jesus promised (John 10 v 10). And if over time neither our desperate prayers nor our diligent work seem to be producing the desired result, we can begin to doubt the "who" that we've been calling on for our "what". Is God really good? Is he able to meet our needs? Is he worth sticking with if he's not going to come through for us? We'll look at these questions in detail in the following chapters, but first let's stand back and spend some time looking at this God in whom Paul found such joyful contentment. Who is he? What is he like?

THE GOD OF WONDERS

"In the beginning God created the heavens and the earth" (Genesis 1 v 1).

Wow. That's quite an opening line, isn't it? The first thing the Bible wants us to know about God is that he created everything. Absolutely everything.

Sun, moon, stars. Earth, wind, sky. Land and sea. Animals, vegetables and minerals. Everything.

I find that all too big to comprehend. For some people, looking up at the stars is a sure-fire way to remind themselves of the glory and majesty of God. For me, it's just too big and distant. (Plus, I live in a city, so it's hard to see more than a few stars on even the clearest nights.) So try this instead. Look at an object near you—it could be this book, or the electronic device you're reading it on, or maybe the chair you're sitting in.

God made that object; he made all the materials that go into it. He gave them their properties: hard, soft, solid, liquid, rigid, flexible, cold, warm. He made the tools that harvested, mined, collected or manufactured the materials. He made the hands of all the people whose work went into taking those materials and forming them into that object. He made the minds of those who invented it, and of those who crafted it. He made your eyes to see it, your fingers to touch it, the complex system of nerve endings and brain synapses that enables you to look at or touch something and know whether it is hard or soft, hot or cold, wet or dry. Without him, none of that would be possible. Amazing.

Here's another incredible thing he invented: the water cycle. Think about that for a moment. Not only did God come up with the idea of water, but he gave it important properties. In its liquid state, water flows downhill and finds its way to the lowest point possible. Most things, once they reach the bottom of a hill, will stay there until moved by some external force. But God designed water's molecular structure so that it also evaporates—rising up into the sky, floating around for a while, and falling down somewhere new. If God hadn't designed water to act like that, we would be living in a world of desert mountains rising out of stagnant swamps. Instead, H_2O keeps flowing round and round, up and down, bringing freshness and life instead of the stale reek of death.

And because water is his creation and he can do what he likes with it, sometimes God plays with its properties: he can turn water into wine (John 2 v 1-11) or blood (Exodus 7 v 14-24). He can make it stand up in a heap (Joshua 3 v 9-16) or lie down and be still (Mark 4 v 35-41). He can make it solid enough to walk on (Matthew 14 v 22-33) or cause it to pour out of a rock (Exodus 17 v 1-6). So whatever you feel that you're missing in life, know this: it is not because God is powerless to act for you.

Yet as amazing as anything in God's creation is, it is as nothing to the wonder of who he is. It was after one of these water miracles, the calming of the storm, that Jesus' disciples first began to get a sense of who they had been travelling around with all that time:

That day when evening came, [Jesus] said to his disciples, "Let us go over to the other side." Leaving the crowd behind, they took him along, just as he was, in the boat. There were also other boats with him. A furious squall came up, and the waves broke over the boat, so that it was nearly swamped. Jesus was in the stern, sleeping on a cushion. The disciples woke him and said to him, "Teacher, don't you care if we drown?"

He got up, rebuked the wind and said to the waves, "Quiet! Be still!" Then the wind died down and it was completely calm.

He said to his disciples, "Why are you so afraid? Do you still have no faith?"

They were terrified and asked each other, "Who is this? Even the wind and the waves obey him!" (Mark 4 v 35-41)

Notice that last verse; it was *after* Jesus calmed the storm that the disciples got really scared. This was power beyond anything they had ever imagined. Before, the worst outcome they were expecting was death. Now they discovered they were sharing an enclosed space with a power far greater. They were standing feet away from a man who could control the most untameable forces of the universe with a quiet word. And their lives were in his hands. No wonder they were terrified.

WHEN FEAR MEETS LOVE

Fear is an appropriate response to seeing who God is. In Revelation 1 v 9-18 the apostle John saw a vision of Christ in all his holiness and might, and it caused him to fall to his knees. Centuries earlier, when Isaiah saw a vision of God's throne room, it caused him to tremble with fear as he recognised his sinfulness (Isaiah 6 v 1-5). When we begin to see God for who he is, we start to understand more about who we are—and to realise we don't come out so well. As the psalmist put it:

> *When I consider your heavens,*
> *the work of your fingers,*
> *the moon and the stars,*
> *which you have set in place,*
> *what is mankind that you are mindful of them,*
> *human beings that you care for them? (Psalm 8 v 3-4)*

When we see God as *he* is, it enables us to see ourselves as *we* are—which is to say, pretty small. We find that we don't quite hold the exalted, central position in our lives that we thought we did. Like John, we are struck down by our own insignificance. But it gets worse. When we contemplate God's total purity, then, like Isaiah, we become aware of our sinfulness, acutely conscious of all our faults and failings.

And yet, miraculously, wonderfully, amazingly, in the next instant we discover God's overwhelming love for us. After asking, "What is mankind that you are mindful of them?"—*Who are we that you would even notice us?*—the psalmist marvels:

> *You have made them a little lower than the angels*
> *and crowned them with glory and honour.*
> *You made them rulers over the works of your hands;*
> *you put everything under their feet. (Psalm 8 v 5-6)*

This isn't just someone noticing us and caring for us; this is the God of the universe endowing us with lavish, abundant dignity and worth. He has chosen human beings to bear his image. He has crowned us—though so unworthy—with glory and honour. He has entrusted us with ruling his creation. All the molecules in that object you were thinking about earlier—they are under your authority in your privileged position as a human being.

God has allowed us to split atoms and to temper steel. He has given us the power to cut down forests and to plant vineyards. He has permitted us to touch the moon and explore the depths of the ocean. We can't (yet) make a hurricane die down at will, but we can harness the wind's energy to light our homes, heat our food and power our entertainment. Nor can we yet turn water into wine or blood. But God has given us the freedom to keep trying, and the brains to work out how we might do these things.

And yet, in a way, it is this very act of endowing us with power and authority that can cause God to be diminished in our eyes. We so easily forget the source of our abilities and think it's all down to us. It's only when things go wrong and we don't get the outcomes we long for that we realise the limits of our humanity: when we can't make someone fall in love with us; when, even with all the scientific advances of fertility treatment, we can't create the child we long for; when we can't cure every disease or prevent every tragedy. When we reach the limits of our power, we turn to God for his.

And when he says no, or does nothing? It's devastating.

If he *can* do it, why doesn't he? Doesn't he care?

That's why we need to know that God isn't just powerful; he is love. We see it throughout the Old Testament:

The LORD, the LORD, the compassionate and gracious God, slow to anger, abounding in love and faithfulness, maintaining love to thousands, and forgiving wickedness, rebellion and sin. (Exodus 34 v 6-7)

*I have loved you with an everlasting love;
    I have drawn you with unfailing kindness.*

(Jeremiah 31 v 3)

*From everlasting to everlasting
    the LORD's love is with those who fear him.*

(Psalm 103 v 17)

And this is not some abstract, distant, generalised love. This is personal. He doesn't just love from afar; he came down and lived among us and loved us with his whole being in the person of Christ.

For God so loved the world that he gave his one and only Son, that whoever believes in him shall not perish but have eternal life. (John 3 v 16)

When [Jesus] saw the crowds, he had compassion on them. (Matthew 9 v 36)

But God demonstrates his own love for us in this: while we were still sinners, Christ died for us. (Romans 5 v 8)

Christ loved us and gave himself up for us.

(Ephesians 5 v 2)

This is how God showed his love among us: he sent his one and only Son into the world that we might live through him. This is love: not that we loved God, but that he loved us and sent his Son as an atoning sacrifice for our sins.
(1 John 4 v 9-10)

He loves you, he loves you, he loves you. I can't state that strongly enough. He loves you. Not just as his image-bearer (although that would be more than enough). If you're a Christian, God loves you as his child.

And that love cost him. The God of heaven took on flesh and humbled himself to rescue you from the jaws of hell. God the Son—"through [whom] all things were made; without [whom] nothing was made that has been made" (John 1 v 3)—stepped into his creation to save it.

The hands that formed humanity submitted themselves to the hands of his creatures. A tree that he grew was cut down and formed into his instrument of execution. Iron that he had threaded into the depths of the earth was dug up and formed into nails which were pounded through his hands and feet. Thorns that he had invented were woven into a mocking crown and forced onto his head. The nerve endings he had designed cried out in anguish. His created ones lifted him high, but only to humiliate the one they should have worshipped. And yet, in love, he cried out, "Father, forgive" (Luke 23:34).

Before you loved him, before you even knew him, he gave up his life for you. Never doubt that this powerful, mighty, holy, awesome God loves you. He may not have given you your "what" yet, but he has given you his "who"—himself.

THE GOD WHO IS

And yet, if we're honest, the questions still remain. If he can do immeasurably more than all we ask or imagine (Ephesians 3 v 20) and he *does* love us, how do we process that when it seems he is withholding good things from us?

It's ok to ask those questions, and even to ask them of God. That's what Mary and Martha did when their brother Lazarus died. In John 11 we read that the sisters sent for Jesus when Lazarus was sick, but Jesus delayed in coming. When he got there, Lazarus was already dead. Both of the grieving sisters greeted Jesus with the same words: "Lord, if you had been here, my brother would not have died" (John 11 v 21, 32). In other words, *You've let us down. You had the power to fix this and you didn't.*

Jesus didn't rebuke them for their honest, hurt responses. Nor did he explain himself. Instead, he revealed something of himself to each of them. With Martha he engaged intellectually and theologically. He told her that her brother would rise again. And when Martha affirmed that she believed in the resurrection of believers at the end of time (v 24), Jesus declared, "*I am* the resurrection and the life ... Do you believe this?" (v 25-26). It was a big claim! Yet with great faith and deep insight, Martha answered, "Yes, Lord ... I believe that you are the Messiah, the Son of God, who is to come into the world" (v 27). Had she ever really thought that through before? It's entirely possible that she hadn't until she was pushed to dig deep and decide who she thought Jesus was.

With Mary, on the other hand, Jesus engaged emotionally: "When Jesus saw her weeping, and the Jews who had come along with her also weeping, he was deeply moved in spirit and troubled … Jesus wept" (v 33, 35).

To Martha the answer to the question *Why didn't you help?* was "I am". To Mary it was *I care.*

Very often, these are the only answers we get, too. Yet throughout Scripture we see that those answers are enough. When Job asked why God had taken his family, his home and his livestock from him, God's answer was effectively, *I am amazing.*

> *Where were you when I laid the earth's foundation?*
>   *Tell me, if you understand.*
> *Who marked off its dimensions? Surely you know!*
>   *Who stretched a measuring line across it?*
> *On what were its footings set,*
>   *or who laid its cornerstone—*
> *while the morning stars sang together*
>   *and all the angels shouted for joy? …*
>
> *Do you give the horse its strength*
>   *or clothe its neck with a flowing mane?*
> *Do you make it leap like a locust,*
>   *striking terror with its proud snorting?*
>   *(Job 38 v 4-7; 39 v 19-20)*

God goes on to spend the whole of chapter 41—a total of 34 verses—talking about how wonderful a sea creature called the Leviathan is! The point is to remind Job of God's incredible power, authority and creativity—and this, ultimately, is the answer Job gets. It's not the answer he expects, but it is the answer he needs.

God's response to our "why" questions is rarely a direct explanation; it's more often a revelation or reminder of his character and capability. And that is because the source of our happiness, joy and contentment can only be found in relationship with him.

That's what the apostle Paul had discovered. For much of his ministry he was imprisoned, often chained night and day to Roman soldiers. He was beaten many times, was separated from his family and friends, and owned little but the clothes on his back... yet the book of Philippians is overflowing with praise and thanksgiving. No matter how bad his circumstances, these could not shake his joyful contentment.

How was this possible? Was Paul some super-Christian, blessed with a double dose of optimism? I don't think so. In Philippians 4 v 12 he says, "I have *learned* the secret of being content in any and every situation" (my emphasis). This wasn't simply his natural demeanour; it was a capacity he had learned, and we can learn it too.

The first step is learning to put the almighty "who" before our pressing "whats". He is always powerful, loving, holy and worthy of our praise. Next time you notice yourself getting caught up in chewing over the "whats" of life—what you want, what you need, what you wish was different—catch that thought. Press the pause button on it, and spend some time focusing on the "who"—on who God is, and who he has made you to be.

Sarah's story

God in the waiting

When I was 18 I was told that it was unlikely that I would be able to have children. I was a committed Christian already, so I decided to trust God with it and genuinely felt, "If God wants me to have children, I'll have children".

I met and married Andy in my twenties, and about a year into marriage we decided to try for a family. Months turned into a year, and when we eventually went for testing to see what was going on, it was indeed confirmed that I wouldn't be able to conceive without the help of some fertility treatment.

Initially we didn't sense a united peace about pursuing fertility treatments—so prayerfully we spent a full decade "trying" without medical intervention. We focused on prayer, we tried fasting, we tried switching to organic diets... you name it, we tried it!

For the first part of that decade we were full of hope—we really believed God would "do" something physical. We had lots of nearlys, almosts, maybes… lots of mountaintop moments and even more valley moments. Our church at times felt very child focused, and that caused a lot of pain. We faced endless questions like, "When will you be having children?" or "Why are you waiting so long to start a family?" We realised that there needed to be some help for people in our situation. So we began to plan a retreat day of teaching, encouragement and prayer for couples facing infertility, which went on to become an annual event. We call it "The Rhythm of Hope" (www.rhythmofhope.co.uk).

We did it because we wanted to reach out amidst our own pain and unresolved situation to encourage others. What we didn't know at the time was that this was happening towards the end of our infertility journey, as God was about to do something unexpected…

Our wonderful and much-awaited son Ezra was born around three years after we ran the first Rhythm of Hope day, 10 years after we started trying for a baby, and 20 years after that first appointment with a fertility specialist when I was 18 years old.

Much as we are overjoyed, our story isn't actually about Ezra. As precious as he is, there is so much more that we gleaned and gained in that decade. Through all the highs and real lows—that complete rollercoaster cycle every month of spending two weeks being so hopeful, then two weeks of being so acutely disappointed—over time we reached a point of real contentment and peace, where we were able to say, "Even if we never have a baby of our own,

God is still good, and we are going to wholeheartedly cling to that".

In all those years of such disappointment and heartache and pain we found God to be so present and so personal and so perfect. He was so incredibly loyal in his love for us as individuals and as a couple. Our worship became so much more intimate, and our time with God became so much more precious. It was raw, but it was real.

Ezra is wonderful. He is our gift, and we are daily grateful; but our testimony is that God is in the waiting and that he is completely good, and ever sovereign over us. Regardless.

Chapter 2

IS GOD GOOD?

I was talking to someone recently about a tricky situation she was going through, where it didn't look as though things were going to turn out the way she had hoped. As we talked about knowing that God is in charge, she remarked, "And of course, his way often turns out to be best after all". She immediately noticed what she had said and corrected herself: "Well, his way is always the best..."

That's where many of us are at if we're honest. Although we know the "right" answer is "God is good; his ways are best", deep down we struggle to believe it—or are slightly surprised when we discover it to be true in "real life".

We've seen that God is the incredible Creator. He is the mighty, powerful King with authority over all our lives. And he loves us, with a mind-blowing sacrificial love. And the Bible is unequivocal about the fact that God is good (1 Chronicles 16 v 34, Psalm 34 v 8, Psalm 107 v 1, Nahum 1 v 7, Luke 18 v 19... and many more). If you grew up in church, this is probably a truth you were taught and have sung about since you were tiny.

But it is possible to know all that yet still worry that perhaps his way isn't the best *for us*. Where does this doubt come from? The problem, at least in part, is that God's idea of good looks very different from ours.

THE GOOD LIFE

We tend to think that a good God would be one who did everything we wanted. Not the sinful things, of course, but the things that make us happy and give us a comfortable life. He himself says he knows how to give good gifts to his children (Matthew 7 v 11). He said he came to give us "life ... to the full" (John 10 v 10)—to give us "the good life". Pause for a moment and think what that would look like for you. What's your idea of "the good life"?

For me that mental picture involved a husband in some kind of church ministry. We'd have four children, who I always imagined playing happily in the overgrown back garden of our old, characterful house.

To the 21st-century Western mind "the good life" often translates to freedom—the ability to go wherever we want and do whatever we want without limits. It looks like prosperity—a nice house, exotic holidays and good schools for the kids. It means self-actualisation—the opportunity to explore and become our true selves. And it means having all our desires met, preferably within 24 hours.

We all have our own definitions of good. But the truth is that it is *God* who gets to define what is good. He is good in himself. His goodness exists outside of what he does for us. Deuteronomy tells us "his works are perfect, and all his ways are just. A faithful God who does no wrong, upright and just is he" (32 v 4). His perspective is very different from ours, too:

"For my thoughts are not your thoughts,
neither are your ways my ways,"
declares the LORD.
"As the heavens are higher than the earth,
so are my ways higher than your ways
and my thoughts than your thoughts." (Isaiah 55 v 8-9)

And this is why it is absolutely vital to our pursuit of contentment that we wrestle with this question: "Is God good?"

Often we're tempted to put conditions on God's goodness: "I'll know he's good if he gives me a spouse" or "How can he be good when my children are suffering?". But when we do that, then we're looking for a God made in our own image. We're revealing that we don't really want a God, we want a genie; a servant we can summon at will to bow to our every request, not a God to whom every knee— even mine—must bow. In fact, God says that this focus on getting our way, having our needs met and our desires fulfilled is actually idolatry—it's a worship of ourselves and our comfort, not of him.

In our culture it's hard to comprehend how a God who requires our worship can be good. We are very wary of those in power who demand obedience and adoration—

and rightly so. Unchecked power in the hands of a human leader is a very dangerous thing. No matter how good the intentions they start out with, there comes a point when their power begins to corrupt them and they start pursuing their own interests at the expense of their people's.

But God is not like that. He demands our worship not only because he is worthy of it, but also for our good, and for our joy! The psalmist discovered this, and wrote, "You make known to me the path of life; you will fill me with joy in your presence, with eternal pleasures at your right hand" (Psalm 16 v 11). In the words of the Westminster Shorter Catechism—a 17th-century statement of faith— our whole purpose, and therefore the way we will find greatest fulfilment, is "to glorify God, and to enjoy him for ever". This is what we were made for—this is our true self-actualisation.

God is good. He promises to give us life to the full—and ultimately he gets to define what that looks like. But notice the sentence that comes before that famous promise of Jesus: "The thief comes only to steal and kill and destroy; I have come that they may have life, and have it to the full" (John 10 v 10). We have a loving Father who is actively seeking to bring us joy, and a deadly enemy who is actively seeking to destroy our joy. And yet so often we choose to believe the lies of the enemy over the promises of God. It's a tale as old as time.

IN THE BEGINNING

Way, way back, when the earth was young, God created Adam. He gave him the whole world to live in, to tend and to rule over. And he gave him one single rule: don't eat from the tree of the knowledge of good and evil, or you will die (Genesis 2 v 17). He then created Eve, a perfect partner for Adam, and they all lived happily ever after...

Until one fateful day. A wily snake sidled up to Eve and asked, "Did God really say, 'You must not eat from any tree in the garden'?" (Genesis 3 v 1). With those words, the very first seed of doubt was sown. No one had ever questioned God before. And here was one of his creatures asking Eve to think about why God was withholding something good. The conversation continued:

> *The woman said to the snake, "We may eat fruit from the trees in the garden, but God did say, 'You must not eat fruit from the tree that is in the middle of the garden, and you must not touch it, or you will die.'"*
>
> *"You will not certainly die," the snake said to the woman. "For God knows that when you eat from it your eyes will be opened, and you will be like God, knowing good and evil."*
>
> *When the woman saw that the fruit of the tree was good for food and pleasing to the eye, and also desirable for gaining wisdom, she took some and ate it. She also gave some to her husband, who was with her, and he ate it.*
> *(Genesis 3 v 2-6)*

Adam and Eve had literally everything they had ever wanted, including total intimacy with God. But the enemy drew their focus to the one thing in the whole universe that they were not allowed to have. He caused them to look at it, to long for it, and then to doubt God's goodness if he was withholding it from them. What a feat of deception! The snake led Adam and Eve from idea to idolatry in six short verses! Advertising executives have got nothing on him. And his tactic is exactly the same today.

We may not live in Eden, but we live in a world in which we are used to being able to get our hands on pretty much whatever we want, any time of the day or night, often without leaving the house. Same-day grocery deliveries, Amazon Prime, Netflix, Uber Eats... we can literally sit in our homes and have a fleet of staff bring us food, books, movies, music, electronics, furniture and anything else we might desire. So when we find God delaying in granting our every request, it takes us by surprise. Sometimes it can be as hard to be content in plenty as in great need— even Paul said he had had to learn the secret of being content "whether living in plenty or in want" (Philippians 4 v 12). Our enemy is determined to convince us that we could be happy, fulfilled and contented if only we had just one more thing—anything, as long as it isn't Jesus.

Like the fruit from the forbidden tree, it could be a good thing in itself—health, friendship, work. It could be justice or freedom or the salvation of a loved one. For me, it was marriage. In my early 20s I had always assumed it was just around the corner, so when the years started to tick by with no knight in shining armour anywhere in sight, I began to wonder what God was doing. The "issue" grew and grew in my mind until, although I was aware of all the very good things in my life, the thing that captured my focus, day after day, was my one area of lack, my "If only".

In what area of your life do you tend to think, "I could be contented if only *this* were different"? Whatever it is, the point is the same: the enemy wants you to see *that* as the source of your discontentment, and to see getting it as the only possible source of contentment. And if you hadn't even been thinking of it, he's going to make sure he draws your attention to it.

We tend to picture the scene in Genesis 3 as taking place around the tree, with Adam and Eve gazing longingly into its branches, but there's no biblical reason to suppose that's where they were when the conversation began. I suspect they were happily minding their own business tending some other part of the garden. There was plenty to be getting on with, and miles of wondrous beauty to explore; why hang around near the one bit you can't partake of? So when the snake asked his question, he brought Eve's attention back to the thing she maybe hadn't given a thought to for weeks.

Once he'd captured her attention, his lies began. First a flat-out contradiction of God's word ("You will not certainly die", v 4), then a suggestion that if the rule wasn't for their protection, it must be because there was some good that

God wanted to withhold from them ("For God knows that when you eat from it your eyes will be opened, and you will be like God, knowing good and evil", v 5). So having thought about the tree, and having begun to question God's goodness, Eve went to have a look: "When the woman saw that the fruit of the tree was good for food and pleasing to the eye, and also desirable for gaining wisdom, she took some and ate it" (Genesis 3 v 6). How she could tell just by looking that the fruit was "good for food" I don't know, but she apparently did. It looked good, the results the serpent promised were good, so she ate.

You don't need me to tell you the consequences.

Eve shows us how dangerous it is when we start to doubt that God is good—when we look at our circumstances, and the limitations on them, and conclude that God must not have our best interests at heart. Eve had everything she could possibly want—the world's best husband, a delightful place to live, bountiful food to pluck from the trees or pull from the ground with the minimum of effort—but one moment of doubting God's goodness was enough to ruin it all for ever, for everyone.

Doubt gave birth to discontentment, discontentment opened the door to temptation, and temptation, when surrendered to, led inevitably to disaster.

Don't be led into a similar trap. When you hear the whisper of lies—through the adverts on TV, the words of a well-meaning friend, the voice in your own head—

telling you that you need more, better, NOW... capture that thought. Unpick the lies about God that lurk behind these assumptions: what does the fact that you want this so badly tell you about how you think he's deficient? And be pro-active too: write down some reminders of God's goodness, put them in a visible place, and practise telling yourself the truth about who he is and what he is like, regardless of your circumstances or your feelings. Choose to rejoice daily in the truth about him: he is good, he is powerful, and he loves you.

WHAT TO DO WITH YOUR DOUBTS

It's one thing to have plenty of good things and find ourselves longing for just one more... But maybe that's not your situation. Maybe you're living through some genuinely bad circumstances. So when you consider the question "Is God good?", you find it hard to say "yes".

Don't mishear me. Doubt is not necessarily sinful. Questioning God is not wrong. It's what we do with that doubt that sets us on a path towards or away from God. The missionary Elisabeth Elliot put it like this:

The psalmist asked why. Job, a blameless man, suffering horrible torments on an ash heap asked why. It does not seem to me to be sinful to ask the question. What is sinful is resentment against God and his dealings with us. When we begin to doubt his love and imagine that he is cheating us of something we have a right to, we are as guilty as Adam and Eve were guilty ... The same snake comes to us repeatedly with the same suggestions: Does God love you? Does he really want the best for you? Is his word trustworthy? ... Forget his promises. You'd be better off if you do it your way. (*Keep a Quiet Heart*, p 44-45)

What could Eve have done with her doubts? She could have turned to Adam and asked him to confirm what God had actually said. And God was not far off. Eve could easily have called to him and asked him to explain. Instead she decided, in the face of overwhelming evidence to the contrary, that the snake, not her Creator, was the one to be trusted. And she put her theory to a tragic test.

Why oh why didn't she ask God for an explanation? Perhaps she had already decided in her heart that she wanted to eat the fruit, and didn't want to be told "no". A former boss of mine, when he wanted to do something he wasn't sure would be allowed, used to say, "It's easier to ask forgiveness than permission", and do it anyway. Perhaps that was Eve's philosophy, too. If so, it was a bad miscalculation. Forgiveness would not come cheap.

But forgiveness *would* come. Once again, God would prove himself to be good. In the aftermath of the man and woman's sin, he was just, meting out appropriate punishment on each of the parties. He was loving, driving Adam and Eve away from the tree of life so they would not have to live for ever under the curse they had brought upon themselves (v 22). And he was kind, making clothes out of animal skin to provide a covering to hide their shame (v 21). In doing so he gave a foretaste of the covering for their sin that he would one day bring about through Jesus.

And that is the ultimate proof of his goodness. The Bible is full of declarations about God's character, but the clearest, most concrete evidence that he is good is that when we disobeyed him, he paid the price. Even as Adam and Eve's sin cut him to the heart, the Father was setting in place his plans to reconcile them and us to himself, through sending his own Son to die on the cross. No matter what we have or don't have, no matter how long and hard the road we're travelling, we have a Saviour who understands, because he has been there too—and he died and rose again so that every hard road will have an end point. The cross is the ultimate demonstration of his character, the clinching proof that he is for us, and the guarantee that one day we will be restored to perfect relationship with him in a new creation that will be better than the first. It is all a gift; it is all undeserved.

Even when we hurt him in the worst possible ways—when we distrust him, dishonour him and disobey him—he is, and remains, good.

THE GOD WE NEED

So what does it look like to wrestle with doubts about God's goodness in a way that means you come out the other side with a more confident faith? Like Sarah and Andy, whose story began this chapter, Sheridan and Merryn Voysey have also experienced childlessness. Sheridan has

41

written a book about their journey, focusing particularly on the year, a decade after they first began trying for a baby, when they decided the time had come to allow that dream to die, and to live wholeheartedly in whatever God had for them instead. The book is called *Resurrection Year*. It is a very raw, honest and beautiful description of what it looks like to wrestle with why a good God would withhold a good gift from good people (not that they would ever call themselves that).

They didn't get any answers. In fact, that was one of the hardest things for them; if God was going to reject their pleas, surely the least he could do was talk to them about it? Isn't that what a good father is like?

In September 2010, Merryn wrote in her journal:

Almost more difficult than the infertility has been the constant silence of God. It's plain courtesy to answer someone's email. We've been sending them to God for ten years and getting no reply.

(Sheridan Voysey, *Resurrection Year*, p 106)

She then read Philip Yancey's book *Disappointment with God*. She explains:

Yancey uses the example of his friend Richard, who lost his faith after a bunch of bad experiences. Richard had three questions about God through his ordeal: is God unfair, is God silent, and is God hidden? Richard's idea was that if only God would reveal himself, speak clearly, and treat people as they deserve, then he could believe ... But Yancey goes on to say that God treated the Israelites just the way Richard wanted, during the Exodus. He was visible to them ... And he spoke clearly to them ... And he treated people fairly through the covenant, with the consequences of breaking it clearly spelled out and agreed to by them beforehand. God was visible, he spoke and he was fair, but the result wasn't the Israelites' faith but their disobedience.

(*Resurrection Year*, p 108)

In other words, sometimes we think, "If God was really good, he would act like this, and then it would be easy to trust him". But trust always requires faith. God can be speaking loud and clear, performing miracles like raining manna and quail down on his people day after day, keeping all his promises, yet the slippery serpent's voice of doubt can still be shouting down the evidence. Under the new covenant God has done a greater miracle for us than those the Israelites witnessed. He has spoken to us through his Son; he has declared his goodness at the cross and the resurrection; he has come to dwell in us by his Spirit. Yet still the voice of doubt seeks to undo our contentment.

This is something we need to be aware of. If we ever find ourselves putting conditions on God's goodness, we *have* to remember it is not the voice of reason speaking, but that of the enemy—the roaring lion who is seeking to devour us. We have to counter his roars by drowning them out with truth, just as God did with Job. Sheridan reflected:

When God broke his silence to Job, he told him nothing about the cause or purpose of his suffering. God simply displayed himself as the all-powerful, all-knowing, majestic creator of the world who is intimately involved in its working. And that was enough for Job. "My ears had heard of you, but now my eyes have seen you."

God rewarded Job but never answered his questions.

Job encountered God and no longer needed answers.
(*Resurrection Year*, p 121-122)

It could happen that God will come to you powerfully, as he did to Job, so that you find all your questions resolved in a moment. You might be so overwhelmed by his goodness, power and majesty that you find it in your heart to trust him unreservedly from that moment on and never look back.

That's how it happened for me with my shortness.

You probably can't tell from reading this, but I'm quite short, and it used to really bother me. I could never see anything in church, at the theatre or at events; I always had to stand in the front row of every photo—feeling exposed, ridiculous and ashamed. Then one weekend our youth group went to a Christian festival somewhere. As ever, I was stuck behind the tallest people in the arena, trying to sing praises to God but unable to see the words on the giant screens a few rows in front, and I was fed up. Then suddenly I began to picture God, seated on his throne, with Jesus standing by his side. They were inviting me in, and Jesus moved towards me to invite me to come closer—and he was exactly my height. He looked me straight in the eyes, without having to bend or crouch, without me having to tip my head back and peer up against the light.

He didn't say anything, and the picture soon faded. I became aware of the venue again, and my brother beside me giving me an odd look, and tears streaming down my face. In that moment I knew I was known, seen, accepted, loved. I was short compared to my friends, but I was the exact height God intended, and he was exactly the God I needed for my life.

I still have to manage my day-to-day life—bathroom mirrors are usually too high, I need a step-ladder to reach the higher shelves in my kitchen, and I still have to stand in the front row of every group photo. But the pain has gone out of it. I have never once since that day felt discontented, cheated or distressed by my height, or lack thereof. As he did with Job, God showed me who he was, and that was enough.

But it doesn't always happen that way. Learning contentment with my singleness was much more a case of what Eugene Peterson has called "a long obedience in the same direction"—a daily choice to trust God whatever my circumstances. We choose, day after day, year after year, to fix our eyes on Jesus, "the pioneer and perfecter" or "author and finisher" (KJV) of our faith (Hebrews 12 v 2). We remind ourselves of who he is, and we choose to believe that he is good, and that therefore, no matter how bad our circumstances feel to us, his ways must also be good.

It is now seven years since *Resurrection Year* was published. Merryn completed a PhD and is now Dr Merryn Voysey. Sheridan has a thriving career as a presenter, author, speaker and journalist. They still don't have children, though they do own a very adorable dog. Those things don't remove the pain of their infertility—no dog, doctorate or dream job can ever fill that hole; and we'll look more at that in the next chapter. They have found, however, that God is good. His goodness is not conditional on his gifts. It is a constant, and it can sustain us when everything else seems hopeless.

Do you believe that? Why not talk to him about it now. Ask him to help you to see his goodness in the world around you and in all that he has done for you.

Rachel's story
The strength of my heart

M y husband Andrew and I have three children: Zeke (11), Anna (9) and Samuel (4). Zeke was always a bit behind developmentally, but when he was two and a half, he started regressing—losing language and motor skills instead of developing them—and was eventually diagnosed with autism. That same summer Anna started having seizures, and she was also later diagnosed with autism. By the time she reached two and a half, she too had started severely regressing.

One evening during that time, Andrew and I went for a walk. I sat looking out at the sea just begging God for Anna's regression to stop. But it didn't. It continued for another six months. Seven years later, that is still one of the most confusing unanswered prayers to me. As time has gone on we have found it easier to see the goodness of God to us, and we can see it for Zeke in his situation. But for Anna, although there are moments when we can see so much joy in her, it has been hard to understand God's purposes.

We have had to depend on God and rely on him for provision, for the children's safety, for specific health and care services, or just for sleep. It has made us cry out to him more, and helped us understand what it means to thirst for God. For a while it was as if I hungered and thirsted to see the children's development, but now the thirst for God has actually become stronger than the thirst for their development. Development will never satisfy. I used to think, "Just the next milestone, the next milestone, and that will be enough", but you're never really satisfied with that. Just like you're never satisfied in any part of life—you're always reaching for "one more" of that thing, or one more milestone. But that is an echo of our real thirst, which is actually for God. If I can satisfy myself in God, I can be much more content on a daily basis because I have that real thirst satisfied.

Going through this struggle has given me faith that God satisfies my soul with good things, even if those good things aren't the things I expected. Our life is so full of joy. Even if the joy isn't in the context that we expected, he has satisfied our soul with good things.

He is enough—not that I don't still cry, or feel pain, but he is enough to console and comfort and to give eternal hope rather than just a trite promise of a bright tomorrow. At my most shaky moments I have clung to Psalm 73, where it says, "My flesh and my heart *may* fail, but God is the strength of my heart and my portion for ever" (v 26, emphasis added). There have been days when I've felt that my flesh and my heart were about to fail, but at the very core of me there is an anchor that doesn't move, because it's him. We've had to lay down expectations and standards that weren't easy to surrender, but ultimately at the core he is the strength of my heart and my portion for ever. And that is enough.

———

Rachel and Andrew Wilson are the authors of *The Life You Never Expected* (IVP UK, 2015), published in the US as *The Life We Never Expected* (Crossway, 2016).

Chapter 3

IS GOD ENOUGH?

"I'm just not cut out to be single." The friend who said that to me was part of a large, thriving church, with plenty of single Christians, but hadn't found a potential husband there. She had tried the Christian dating websites, and had no success there. She was tired of being on her own. Her solution? To give up on looking for a Christian boyfriend and try the secular dating sites instead.

Her heartfelt phrase has stuck with me. It breaks my heart, because look at what it implies. Who created her—who "cut her out"? Who has the power to bring people into her life, or arrange things so they never quite meet? Who gave us the parameters for healthy relationships? So what she's saying is: "God created me, and designed me with this need. But he has failed to fulfil it within his parameters, so I'll have to find a way to meet the need outside of his will".

Maybe you've asked a similar question: Why would God create us with a need and then withhold the fulfilment of it?

There are only two possible answers to that question. Either God is mean, or he has another way of meeting your need than the one you can see.

That's why we started with the truth of God's goodness. He is not mean. Once we've established that as an eternal, immutable, immovable reality, we can stand on that bedrock and consider the second option. Is it possible that he can meet your need in some other way than the one you're looking for?

DESPERATE TIMES, DANGEROUS MEASURES

When our needs loom so large that we'll do anything to meet them, we're in a dangerous position. That's something we see in the story of Esau:

Once when Jacob was cooking some stew, Esau came in from the open country, famished. He said to Jacob, "Quick, let me have some of that red stew! I'm famished!"

… Jacob replied, "First sell me your birthright."

"Look, I am about to die," Esau said. "What good is the birthright to me?"

But Jacob said, "Swear to me first." So he swore an oath to him, selling his birthright to Jacob.

Then Jacob gave Esau some bread and some lentil stew. He ate and drank, and then got up and left.

So Esau despised his birthright. (Genesis 25 v 29-34)

Esau had a genuine need—he'd been working hard all day and was hungry. But in a moment of weakness Esau chose to prioritise his present need over the future promise of his birthright. So he gave up everything his status as oldest son entailed—his inheritance, his place in God's salvation plan, the promise of God's blessing, his very identity—for the sake of a bowl of lentil stew.

Esau's need was real and significant, but he was willing to pay far too much to meet that need. The last line reveals what his sin was: Esau despised his birthright. Which means he was despising the givers of that right—both his earthly father and his heavenly one—hence why the New Testament describes Esau as "godless" (Hebrews 12 v 16). He looked at his need, and he looked at the cost of meeting it, and decided that all his privileges as the firstborn son were worth less than his lunch. His very temporary, short-term discontentment caused him to lose his perspective on what was really important and throw it all away.

Contrast that with how Jesus handled a similar situation:

Then Jesus was led by the Spirit into the wilderness to be tempted by the devil. After fasting for forty days and forty nights, he was hungry. The tempter came to him and said, "If you are the Son of God, tell these stones to become bread."

Jesus answered, "It is written: 'Man shall not live on bread alone, but on every word that comes from the mouth of God.'" (Matthew 4 v 1-4)

Notice the slightly different scale of the need. We don't know how long Esau had been out hunting for—it's possible that he had been gone for a few days, but unless he was both very ill-prepared and a very poor hunter, he had presumably eaten more recently than forty days ago. Jesus had had nothing but water for forty days. Now his fast was over, he could legitimately have eaten. So why didn't he?

The temptation before Jesus was to question God's word. The last thing that had happened before Jesus went into the wilderness was his baptism, when God declared from heaven: "This is my Son, whom I love; with him I am well pleased" (Matthew 3 v 17).

Forty days later, the first thing the enemy says is, *Are you sure you're God's son? Prove it!* In his classic Bible commentary, the 18th-century minister Matthew Henry explains the temptation this way:

> [The enemy] does not say, *Pray to thy Father* that he would turn them into bread; but *command* it to be done; thy Father hath forsaken thee, set up for thyself, and be not beholden to him.

Or in plain English: *Take matters into your own hands.*

Jesus' response shows us what was at stake here: if he had taken up the tempter's suggestion, he would have been giving up that which was most precious to him— his reliance on his Father—for the sake of a bread roll. Imagine that; after forty days without food, Jesus was still able to say, *God is enough. I trust him to know best and to provide for all my needs.*

Humans were designed with needs. Feeling hungry is not wrong. But there are right ways and wrong ways of going about meeting our needs. Some of these are obviously wrong—a night of binge drinking to drown our sorrows, for example, or looking to someone outside our marriage to fulfil our need for romantic emotional connection. Other times it is less clear whether our actions are right or wrong: where is the line, for instance, between being conscientious and overworking? How do you know whether you are being wise with your money or being miserly?

This is a tricky one, because there are ways in which we have to take action to meet our needs. Paul took on work as a tentmaker in Corinth (Acts 18 v 3), and he, Silas and Timothy instructed the Thessalonian believers that it was right to work to earn your keep (2 Thessalonians 3 v 6-10). So the lesson of the Christian life is not "sit back, relax and God will pour everything you need into your lap". Instead we seek to put the first things first, and understand that work as hard as we might, in the end, the results are up to God.

RAISING AUTISTIC KIDS

Some of us have to learn this the hard way. Andrew and Rachel Wilson, who we met at the start of this chapter, had family life all planned out. But when their children were diagnosed with autism, everything they thought they knew about parenting flew out the window, along with many of their hopes, dreams and even basic expectations. It was no longer a given that their kids would ever learn to drive, go to summer camps, or get married. Zeke and Anna might never be able to live independently.

So Andrew and Rachel got on with their new job: coping. Rachel spent hours every week making appointments with doctors and therapists, chasing up therapeutic equipment that hadn't been delivered, filing claims for financial benefits—and all while caring for children with multiple, complex needs. It was exhausting, and often deeply discouraging.

Nothing Rachel was doing was wrong. Much of it was vitally important. Her children had needs, and as their mother, she was seeking to make sure they were met. But Rachel came to realise that while the actions may have been good, her attitude wasn't; she was acting as though her children's welfare was entirely dependent on human effort.

That is, after all, what our culture constantly tells us: we (humans) are responsible for our children's flourishing. Whether it's parents, teachers, social workers or "the system", if there's a problem, "someone" needs to fix it. Someone needs to ensure that everything possible is done to ameliorate any problems our children may face. So if we don't manage to get the very best equipment and provision right when we need it, we are failures, and probably causing irreparable harm. This is too heavy a burden to carry, even for parents of children who don't have additional needs. The truth is, we're not designed to be able to meet all of another person's needs. We're weak and limited, and that weakness is meant to point us towards God. Rachel puts it like this:

> I could have a rolling schedule of every therapy under the sun ... but if my mind is not settled toward God as the author of it all, and if I am not putting him first, I might as well quit. It will all be in vain; it won't bring me any peace, and the true battle is being lost.
>
> The reverse is true, too. Zeke could be running laps and flapping his hands in one corner, Anna could be wandering in circles and grinding her teeth in another, and the floor between them could look like the results of an explosion in a children's centre. But if, through it all, my thoughts are ordered, and I am able to see my circumstances in a God-shaped way, then the true battle is being won. (*The Life You Never Expected*, p 45)

Rachel is not saying that she shouldn't have bothered to drag Zeke and Anna to all those appointments, to fight to get them into a special school, or to have bought all the specialised equipment. All that stuff is important, but it is peripheral:

> I love my kids most by not loving them the most but by first loving God. As soon as ... I begin to believe that I alone must push for them and control their destinies [or for myself, and control mine], the unbearable weight of playing God soon becomes apparent.

In other words, Rachel is not enough. Only God is enough. Equally, the outcomes Rachel continues to pray for and work towards are desirable, but they are not sufficient to meet either her or her children's real needs.

It is easy to get distracted by the legitimate needs in front of us and forget about the big picture. That was what Esau did. His genuine need for food was enough to distract him from the truth of what his real need was— to be part of God's covenant people, a status symbolised by his birthright. Jesus' need for food was far greater, yet he had his priorities straight; he knew he needed to do all things in submission to his Father, rather than seeking to usurp power.

And those are our biggest needs too. As Jesus told the woman at the well, "Everyone who drinks [earthly] water will be thirsty again, but whoever drinks the water I give them will never thirst" (John 4 v 13-14). Our physical needs are real, but they are also pictures illustrating to us our deepest need of all—our need for Jesus.

The psalmist expresses this in Psalm 42: "As the deer pants for streams of water, so my soul pants for you, my God. My soul thirsts for God, for the living God." Our need for water points us to our need for the living water of Christ's life in us. Our longing for relationships points to our need for fellowship with our Creator. Our needs point us to the ultimate source of all we need, and when we have him, he proves always to be enough.

REAL NEEDS, SURPRISING MEANS

This doesn't mean that God doesn't care about our physical or material needs. But he loves to demonstrate how he can provide for them without all our striving. One famous example of this from history is that of George Mueller, the 19th-century orphanage founder.

"The children are dressed and ready for school. But there is no food for them to eat," the housemother of the orphanage informed George Mueller. George asked her to take the 300 children into the dining room and have them sit at the tables. He thanked God for the food and waited. George knew God would provide food for the children as he always did. Within minutes, a baker knocked on the door. "Mr. Mueller," he said, "last night I could not sleep. Somehow I knew that you would need bread this morning. I got up and baked three batches for you. I will bring it in."

Soon, there was another knock at the door. It was the milkman. His cart had broken down in front of the orphanage. The milk would spoil by the time the wheel was fixed. He asked George if he could use some free milk. George smiled as the milkman brought in ten large cans of milk. It was just enough for the 300 thirsty children. ("George Mueller, Orphanages built by prayer", Christianity.com)

The need was genuine, but instead of rushing round in a panic trying to fix the issue, Mueller chose to put his faith in God, and allow him to provide—and God came through.

If you have real needs, there's nothing wrong with asking God to meet them. From the outright miraculous to the beautifully providential, God provides in very real and concrete ways. Look out for the ways he's looking out for you, and give thanks.

One of the most common ways that God moves to meet our needs is through our church family. In the same letter that Paul speaks of his contentment in Christ, he thanks the Philippian Christians for sending him money (with a slight side-swipe at the other churches that hadn't given him financial aid!) (Philippians 4 v 14-16). James has a stark warning for church families who *don't* meet one another's needs: "Suppose a brother or a sister is without clothes and daily food. If one of you says to them, 'Go in peace; keep warm and well fed,' but does nothing about their physical needs, what good is it?" (James 2 v 15-16). We don't serve one another by simply saying to those in need, "I'm sorry you're hungry, cold, lonely, grieving, afraid, or otherwise in need. Just trust God and all will be well." No, we feed them, clothe them, and bring them into our homes. If you are hungry, cold, lonely, grieving, afraid, or otherwise in need, then look to your church family to be the hands from which God's help comes. For example, if you're struggling to be content with your singleness because you *need* to feel known and loved and accepted by someone, you should be able to find a whole host of someones in your church to meet that need—even if that's a brother or sister, not the spouse you expected.

But at the same time, we must recognise that the physical reality isn't the only reality. After all, there seems to be little rhyme or reason for why God fixes some of our earthly problems and not others. Andrew and Rachel's children still have autism, Sheridan and Merryn Voysey are still childless. Some people receive miraculous healing, others struggle with chronic illness for decades. We don't know why. Yet although God has not removed their problem, he does meet their need. The author Tanya Marlow, who has been housebound with ME (Myalgic Encephalomyelitis) since 2010, puts it like this: "God turns up in our discomfort, and that makes all the difference" (*Those Who Wait*, p 19). He is enough.

FULLNESS OF JOY

So let's get really practical. What is it that you need (or want)? What is the thing about which you think, "If only that were resolved, then I'd be happy" or "Life is fine, but I wish this part of it were different"? What would abundant life look like to you? A spouse? A different spouse? Children? Full health? A better job? A bigger house? A helpful exercise might be to make a list of those things, or to write a description of the life you're longing for, highlighting the bits that you feel are missing. Then think about *why* you want those things—are there deeper needs that lie underneath them? What need are you looking for that house or that spouse to meet? For many of us it is simply a sense that we haven't achieved or acquired the things we thought we would (or should) by this age. Is it a case of broken expectations? What does the enemy tell you that this lack means about who you are and how your life is going?

As the years rolled on for me, the lie the enemy whispered was, "You're not good enough. If you were tall, slim and beautiful you'd have no trouble finding a husband..." He'd even tell me that I wasn't a good enough Christian to find a godly husband. Can you see how the discontentment escalated? It grew from being one missing piece, to unhappiness with my body, my face and even my faith. No husband could ever have changed that narrative. But God could. Over time, he has gently spoken truth to me to counter Satan's lies. He has bound up those broken-hearted wounds (Psalm 147 v 3) and has led me to a place of deep contentment in him. Is it possible that he could do the same for you? Might he be able to meet your deepest needs through other means?

Talk to him about it. Ask him to help you listen to his words of truth and not the enemy's words of deception. Ask him to help you to desire him more than any of the things you lack. He may change your heart overnight, but more likely it will be a process of pressing into him, learning to trust him with the smaller things, finding him faithful, and therefore being willing to open your hand wider and trust him with some of the big things.

As we make the daily choice to run into the open arms of our heavenly Father, we will discover that the things we thought we needed—a home, a family, a fulfilling career, good health—are all just added blessings. They're wonderful, and they're good things, and we're not wrong to want them, but if we begin to think they are things we need in order to be content, we reveal that they have become idols in our lives.

The psalmist puts it like this:

> *Better is one day in your courts*
> *than a thousand elsewhere;*
> *I would rather be a doorkeeper in the house of my God*
> *than dwell in the tents of the wicked. (Psalm 84 v 10)*

Just standing near God's presence, outside the door, was better to the psalmist than all the good things the world could offer. "The wicked" here are simply those who are not followers of the living God. So the psalmist is not saying *I suppose it's better to be somewhere near you than stuck in a hovel with thieves and drug dealers*. He's saying, *I could have whatever I wanted in the world—a home, prestige, friends, money—but all of that is so worthless compared to being with you that even a lowly task in your temple is better than those other riches.*

So, is God enough? Just being near him was enough for the psalmist. In fact, many of the Psalms echo the same sentiment. Consider Psalm 16, for a start: "'You are my Lord; apart from you I have no good thing" (v 2), "Lord, you alone are my portion and my cup" (v 5), "you will fill me with joy in your presence, with eternal pleasures at your right hand" (v 11). And Psalm 73:

JENNIE POLLOCK

Whom have I in heaven but you?
   And earth has nothing I desire besides you.
My flesh and my heart may fail,
   but God is the strength of my heart
        and my portion for ever. ...
As for me, it is good to be near God. (v 25-26, 28)

The theme is echoed in the New Testament. The writer of Hebrews instructed his readers:

Keep your lives free from the love of money and be content with what you have, because God has said, "Never will I leave you; never will I forsake you." (Hebrews 13 v 5)

And once again we see that God's answer to our needs is rarely the thing we asked for, but is most often himself: *Don't worry about X [money, a spouse, a child, your health, your child's health ... whatever]; you've got me.*

The evidence of the Bible is that we can have all the things we thought we needed stripped away, and find that God is the greater treasure. Writing from prison, with no freedom, poor health, no family and few friends close by, Paul reassured the Philippians that: "God will meet all your needs according to the riches of his glory in Christ Jesus" (Philippians 4 v 19). How could Paul say that so confidently? Because he had found it to be true for himself. In all the crazy situations he had been in—beaten, shipwrecked, imprisoned, hungry, lonely, cold, mocked, abandoned, even bitten by poisonous snakes—God was sufficient for all his needs. And not just "sufficient", but plenty. Paul wasn't "just about managing"; he was flourishing.

WHEN THE WELL RUNS DRY

You may not feel as if you're flourishing. You may never have had the kind of experience of God where you *feel* his presence. Others report finding themselves moved to tears or flooded with joy when they pray or read their Bibles, but you feel nothing. Your heart has never been "strangely warmed" as John Wesley, the founder of the Methodist movement, described experiencing. You sing songs that declare to God, "You are my all in all", "Only you can fill my deepest longings", "You're all I want/You're all I've ever needed". But your experience from one Sunday to the next doesn't reflect this.

I've been there too. For much of the time that I was longing for marriage, I was also going through a particularly dry patch in my relationship with God. I'd never had much experience of an emotional or "spiritual" connection with him—the odd moments, maybe, usually characterised by lots of crying. But this season was particularly empty. I still knew he was God, I would still say that I loved him, but I didn't really *feel* much love—either for him or from him.

My encouragement to you, if you're in the same boat, is two-fold. First—you're not alone. We don't all have those overwhelming emotional experiences. If you look up Wesley's journal entry about his heart being "strangely warmed", you'll see that he goes on to say that he didn't feel any sense of overwhelming joy like many people describe. Instead he clung to the assurance of God's promises in the Bible, and to the evidence of God's work in his life as he helped him to overcome sin and temptation. And over time, Wesley's confidence and depth of relationship grew. Steadfast faith is not reliant on fickle feelings. Nor can your feelings save you—only your faith can. Your salvation does not depend on you having miraculous "spiritual moments" in the desert, but on the fact that Jesus triumphed in the desert on your behalf. Put your confidence in his obedience.

The second encouragement is to keep persevering with this goal of finding your contentment in God alone. When I was still looking for God-plus-husband to meet my needs, my spiritual life was a dry, often weary, plod. A wonderful fringe benefit of having laid aside that desire is that God has begun to feel far more consistently present and real to me. But that was not a quick or a pain-free process. I had to be very honest with myself and with God.

Think about what it is that you need at the moment— the dreams and desires you thought about earlier in the chapter. Do you have the courage to begin to hand them over to him? Are you willing to accept that he won't always meet those needs in the way that you want? Could you pray something similar to what I prayed? *I believe you're enough. That's what your word says, and it's what others who have been through far worse than me also say. It has to be true. But, Lord, I don't feel like it's true. I want you-plus-*

something else. Please change my heart so that I willingly put you in your rightful place. Help me to want you more than the thing I really want right now.

That's a scary thing to pray, because it means giving God permission not to give us the thing we've been requesting for so long! But if we want to find joyful contentment, we're going to have to have some of those painful conversations with God, and to let go of the things that are taking his place in our lives.

It took time, and still some days are easier than others, but God has answered my prayer. When I allowed him to be everything, he proved that he really is enough.

Scott and Claire's story
A Kingdom that cannot
be shaken

Scott and Claire Marques live in Harare, the capital of Zimbabwe. As well as running a business, Scott is lead elder at River of Life Church, and heads up a church-planting network in southern Africa. The political situation in Zimbabwe is still very challenging, with inflation at astronomical levels and shortages of many basic necessities, such as electricity...

Claire: We don't have electricity for the majority of the day in Zimbabwe. The electricity will come on between 10pm and 11pm and go off between five and six in the morning. I've felt God using that to challenge me as to what is the source of my joy. When the power comes back on it's crazy how your mood lifts. And I'm really challenged by that—is my joy in Jesus, my living hope, or is it in more worldly things, like the fact that I have electricity?

I'm challenged to cultivate a lifestyle of thanksgiving—to be very aware of being thankful, to seek to be overflowing with thankfulness (Colossians 2 v 7). The word of God is just full of calls to thankfulness. It really struck me the other day when I read Romans 1, where Paul talks about ungodliness in the world and he says people "neither glorified him as God nor gave thanks to him" (Romans 1 v 21). Lack of gratitude really displeases God, because no matter how extreme the circumstances, there's *always* something to be thankful for.

Scott: We're in a political situation where we really expected massive change [when former Prime Minister Robert Mugabe was overthrown], but now it's actually *harder* to live day by day. And you start to think, "there is no hope of this ever changing; it's too deep-rooted, it's too deep-set".

There's a temptation to panic, where you feel, "I can't manage. I can't pay, I can't look after my kids, I can't get food..." In Matthew 6 we are told, "Do not worry, saying, 'What shall we eat?' or 'What shall we drink?' or 'What shall we wear?' ... your heavenly Father knows that you need [these things]. But seek first his kingdom and his righteousness, and all these things will be given to you as well" (v 31-33). That's a theme all the way through the Bible—that as real as this world feels, God's kingdom and *his* righteousness supersede it, and he *promises* to supply our needs. Him promising to fulfil our needs doesn't guarantee a life of roses, but it does mean walking in *his* presence, walking in *his* provision, whatever that may look like.

There's still a temptation to hopelessness, but I find I've been so inspired by Hebrews in that. It was written around the time of Roman Emperor Nero's persecution, when Christians were being impaled on poles and set alight (or would be soon), but the writer hardly addresses that at all. Instead he spends the first ten chapters just pointing people to Jesus and how wonderful he is: *Jesus is better than Abraham. Jesus is better than the High Priest. Jesus is better than all the things we put our hope in.* Then there's a really fascinating bit where the writer says,

You suffered along with those in prison and joyfully accepted the confiscation of your property, because you knew that you yourselves had better and lasting possessions. So do not throw away your confidence; it will be richly rewarded ... Therefore, since we are receiving a kingdom that cannot be shaken, let us be thankful, and so worship God acceptably with reverence and awe.

(Hebrews 10 v 34-35, 12 v 28)

Our hope is not in this world, but in the greater kingdom to come.

Chapter 4

IS GOD WORTH IT?

The Princess Bride may be the greatest adventure film of all time. In it a grandfather tells his grandson an old, old story: Princess Buttercup is in love with a farm boy, Westley. However, she has been tricked into agreeing to marry the evil Prince Humperdinck. The day before the wedding, Humperdinck has Westley killed. At this point the grandson breaks into the narrative insisting his grandfather must have read that wrong. When the grandfather assures him that it's right, he is outraged and demands, "Who kills Prince Humperdinck?"

The boy knew how stories work, you see: the good guy wins; the bad guy gets defeated; so Humperdinck *must* get his comeuppance in the end. What the boy didn't yet appreciate was that often, in the best stories, there first comes a point when all seems lost. For this plot to turn around, it would take a miracle. The boy has just enough faith in his grandfather to allow him to continue reading, to persist with the story even though it seems hopeless.

Sometimes we need the same kind of faith. When we're discontent with our stories or despairing of things ever getting better, we need to trust that it's all going to turn out well—that the ending will be worth the bumps in the middle.

Unlike the first readers of Hebrews that Scott alluded to, we're unlikely to be impaled on spikes for our faith in the near future (at least in the West, though persecution and torture are realities for believers from some backgrounds and in other parts of the world). But for many of us, there comes a point when the Christian walk just seems too hard. Sometimes it feels as if Jesus asks a lot of us—faithfulness, holiness, purity, putting him first in everything—while withholding from us the thing we really long for. For others of us, our area of discontentment isn't really something we can put a finger on and say, "If *that* area was resolved, then I'd be content". It may simply be that we feel like we're dressed in our Sunday best all the time, and we just want to put on a comfy t-shirt and well-worn jeans and relax.

Maybe you've spent months or years trying hard to do God's will, to honour him in your life and to trust him with everything, but you're not sure how much longer you can keep going. The season doesn't end; the issues don't ease. You start to wonder if you should just step away for a while, and meet your needs in your own strength. That might mean giving up waiting for a godly partner and going to non-Christian dating sites to find love, or flirting with that person at work that you know you shouldn't but who makes you feel noticed and appreciated. It might mean fudging the figures on your timesheet or expenses to try to meet your financial needs. Or it might mean bragging about your home or holidays, or posting carefully edited and filtered photos on your social media feeds to try to paint a better image of yourself and your life than the reality.

Even if you haven't *actually* sought to meet your needs through sinful means, you may well have sighed about the restrictiveness of living a godly life: *If only I wasn't a Christian, I could take that opportunity. No one would ever know; it wouldn't really matter. And it would be nice...*

Whatever our temptations to sin are, they are almost always rooted in a desire to take a shortcut to comfort or contentment. The road of faithfulness and obedience looks long and hard—and it is. Jesus made no bones about that. "Whoever wants to be my disciple must deny themselves and take up their cross and follow me", he tells us (Mark 8 v 34).

But if you know the gospel story, you know that the cross is not how it ends. Our Lord Jesus "humbled himself by becoming obedient to death—even death on a cross!" It doesn't get much worse than that. But at the moment when all seemed lost, God did something miraculous... "Therefore God exalted him to the highest place and gave him the name that is above every name, that at the name of Jesus every knee should bow, in heaven and on earth and under the earth, and every tongue acknowledge that Jesus Christ is Lord, to the glory of God the Father" (Philippians 2 v 8-11).

In God's story, humility leads to exaltation, shame leads to glory, death leads to life. And not just for Jesus, but for his faithful followers too. Yes, the present may be deeply painful and look utterly hopeless—but we can trust that it will turn out well. If we belong to Christ, he has won for us an ending beyond our imagining.

OUR FUTURE HOPE

So what does that ending look like?

The book of Revelation, the last book in the Bible, begins with the apostle John seeing a vision of the resurrected Jesus in all his glory. Jesus tells him to write to the seven key churches scattered across Asia Minor (present-day Turkey). Chapters 2 and 3 address each church in turn, with "letters" praising them for the things they were doing well, and rebuking them for their failings. I've always read these letters primarily as guides for how to live, based on the things that are commended and condemned in them. But when I read through them again recently, it was the promises contained in each one that jumped out to me. Using vivid imagery, Jesus makes a promise in each letter to "the one who is victorious". Those who persevere in their faith—not giving into the values, demands and empty promises of their particular culture, but clinging faithfully to Jesus to the end—he calls "victorious". And as in all battles, the victor gets the spoils. God promises great rewards to those who stand firm against the trials and temptations of this world:

To the one who is victorious, I will give the right to eat from the tree of life, which is in the paradise of God. (2 v 7)

To the one who is victorious and does my will to the end, I will give authority over the nations ... I will also give that one the morning star. (2 v 26, 28)

The one who is victorious will ... be dressed in white. I will never blot out the name of that person from the book of life, but will acknowledge that name before my Father and his angels. (3 v 5)

To the one who is victorious, I will give the right to sit with me on my throne, just as I was victorious and sat down with my Father on his throne. (3 v 21)

Think about those for a moment. Are you anxious about ageing or the decay you see in your body? One day you will "eat from the tree of life", and know what it is to be fully alive—perhaps for the first time ever, and certainly for all eternity. Imagine having no fear of sickness or pain; imagine all weariness gone for good. Imagine never comparing your body negatively with anyone else's ever again.

Feeling overlooked or undervalued? One day you will have "authority over the nations". We will reign alongside the God of glory, as joint heirs with his son. We will have the right to sit on Christ's throne, at the right hand of the

Father! No longer will we be wrestling to prove our worth in a world whose targets are ever shifting and whose values conflict with godly ones. We will have power and authority, without any hint of sin to make us wield it unjustly or long for more.

Discontent with your intellect, achievement or opportunities? Concerned about being rejected for not making the grade? You will one day be "dressed in white" garments denoting your honour and purity. What's more, Jesus himself will stand before the Father and all the angels and acknowledge you by name. You will be seen and known and loved. You will be secure. There is no danger that you will ever be rejected or looked down on again. Jesus will never leave you or forsake you (Hebrews 13 v 5).

We are promised riches beyond compare, the intimate relationship we long for, honour and authority. We are also promised things the meaning of which is not so clear: "the morning star", for example (2 v 28), or the "hidden manna" and "white stone" of 2 v 17. If anything, that is even more exciting. Not only are we to be given fulfilment of the things we long for in ways we can already understand and perhaps imagine, but we are to be lavished with gifts whose purpose and worth we can't yet begin to fathom.

And of course, our greatest hope is not just of a future where "there will be no more death or mourning or crying or pain" (Revelation 21 v 4); it's a future where we're *with* the One who brings that about:

Look! God's dwelling-place is now among the people, and he will dwell with them. They will be his people, and God himself will be with them and be their God. "He will wipe every tear from their eyes." (Revelation 21 v 3-4)

Think back to a time of sweet communion with God: a time when you particularly felt the presence of his Spirit or heard him speak through his word; or a time when the good news seemed so good that your heart was bursting with praise. These moments are wonderful, but they're only like catching the smell of something delicious cooking in the kitchen while you're in another room. One day you will feast in full, with all your senses, as you dwell with God in eternity; and when he invites you to the dinner table, all the longing, all the heartache, all the pain, will be gone for good with a brush of his hand on your cheek.

Until that day, we'll sometimes be tempted to give up. In those moments, we have to ask ourselves: do we believe God's way is better, that it is worth the delay to our gratification, that he is worth more than the earthly treasure that has captured our gaze? It is good to be faithful to God simply because it is commanded, of course. But in his incredible kindness, knowing our frailty, he gives us occasional glimpses of the glorious future that he has in store for us, too.

A MEANINGFUL STORY

And he doesn't just tell us about our future hope as a sort of carrot to get us plodding in the right direction, with our eyes fixed on a prize we never quite reach. He does it to help us understand the story we're living in.

One thing that sets humans apart from all other living creatures is that we are "meaning-making" beings. Unlike dogs, cats, dolphins, kangaroos and the rest, we don't simply follow our impulses; instead we seek work, relationships and activities that have a sense of purpose, of meaning. We want to know what life in general, and our life in particular, is all about. What's the point? What is it all for? Without a sense of being part of a greater narrative our lives seem at best impoverished, and at worst completely hopeless.

On the other hand, when we have a narrative of life which gives meaning to the world around us, it can give the most horrific situations a sense of purpose and even hope. The psychologist and Holocaust survivor Viktor Frankl discovered that "the people who survived in concentration camps were not the strongest or the most well-fed or the most muscular, it was the people who had a sense of meaning, which kept them going" (summarised by Mark Sayers in his podcast, *This Cultural Moment*, Season 3 Episode 3).

Stories have power. Having a concept of a bigger picture that we are part of helps us to make sense of life when things don't work out as we had hoped. Any larger narrative can do this. The story is told of two labourers at work. One is wearied and burdened, trudging about his work with heavy feet; the other is cheerful and light-footed. An observer asks the first what he is doing, "I have to move these bricks over there, then mix up this huge pile of sand into cement..." he mutters, resentfully. The observer asks the same question of the second man. "I'm building a cathedral," comes the joyous reply. "It's going to draw people from miles around to worship." The tasks and the burdens were the same, but the second man had grasped the meaning and purpose of it all, while the first man had only seen the bricks.

Knowing that you're building a cathedral can give meaning, at least in the short term. But the Christian story is better by far. It is the true story—the one that makes sense of the whole universe and our experience of it. It is the eternal story—which means we will never reach the end and need to look around for another. We will never plumb the depths of its goodness and richness. Only this story can help us to find lasting, fulfilling contentment when our circumstances are less than ideal.

This is what helped Paul. He encouraged the believers in Corinth by reminding them that "our light and momentary troubles are achieving for us an eternal glory that far outweighs them all" (2 Corinthians 4 v 17). That can sound dismissive, until you remember all the trials Paul had been through—floggings, imprisonment, shipwreck, and general opposition to his message and rejection in many of the places he visited. Paul's experience puts our discontentments with our home, work and relationships into perspective somewhat! He knew what it was to be lonely, to be afraid, to be disappointed, to be in need and to be rejected. He doesn't speak to us as one who doesn't understand. But he tells us of both the present reality of God's sufficiency and the future hope that it will all be worth it in the end.

It's a perspective that still works today, too. I met Scott and Claire Marques, who we heard from at the start of the chapter, when they were speaking at a Christian festival in the UK. They told us about all the challenges they face daily, living in Zimbabwe. Yet what came over most strongly was the sense of joyful contentment that simply bubbled over from them. The more they had lost, it seemed, the more they felt the power of the assurances of hope in passages as Hebrews 10 and 12. We have better and lasting possessions awaiting us in the future than we could ever have on earth. Our confidence in Christ will be richly rewarded. We will inherit—and in fact are already receiving—a kingdom that can never be shaken (see Hebrews 10 v 34-35, 12 v 28). Understanding their part in the bigger picture of what God is doing has been key to them learning the secret of being content.

And it can do the same for you. Whatever your current "If only..." is, whatever plot twists have undermined your confidence, whatever details you wish you could rewrite, don't lose confidence in where the story is going. God has not made a mistake. He hasn't got overwhelmed with all the plates he's trying to keep spinning, and let you fall. There is a plan—a good plan. One day you will be with Jesus, in a perfect new creation, looking back on this part of your story and giving thanks to God that he wrote it exactly how he did. It will make perfect sense. It will have the meaning you are wishing you could discern right now.

FAITH FOR THE LONG-TERM

So what does that mean for us now, in the humdrums and heartaches of the everyday? What does it look like to live in a way that's confident of the ending—that trusts God really will deliver on his promises for eternity? The Old Testament figure of Abraham gives us an example.

When we first meet Abraham and his wife Sarah in Genesis 12, they are an old, childless couple living in a land belonging to others. But then God steps in and invites Abraham into his story of salvation: he promises to make Abraham the father of a great nation, and says that through his offspring the whole world would experience God's blessing (Genesis 12 v 2-3; 17 v 1-22). Sarah was already well past child-bearing age. It looked hopeless, ridiculous even. But a whole 25 years later, God finally gave Abraham and Sarah the son he had promised: Isaac (Genesis 21 v 1-7).

But then a few years later a bewildering thing happened. God said to Abraham, "Take your son, your only son, whom you love—Isaac—and go to the region of Moriah. Sacrifice him there as a burnt offering on a mountain that I will show you" (Genesis 22 v 2). What?! Take his beloved son—the son he had waited so long for, the son on whom the whole grand narrative of his life rested—and sacrifice him? Why would God ask Abraham to give up the very thing God had promised?

This was a test of where Abraham's heart was. God had "come through" for Abraham and given him what he longed for, but had Isaac then taken the place of God in Abraham's life?

The writer of Genesis doesn't tell us what Abraham thought or felt at this point. We can't see the tears in his eyes or the heaviness in his footsteps. What we do know is that "early the next morning Abraham got up and loaded his donkey. He took with him two of his servants and his son Isaac. When he had cut enough wood for the burnt offering, he set out for the place God had told him about" (v 3). He didn't waste time, he didn't hesitate. God commanded, and Abraham obeyed.

When they reached the place God had told him about, Abraham built an altar there and arranged the wood on it. He bound his son Isaac and laid him on the altar, on top of the wood. Then he reached out his hand and took the knife to slay his son. (v 9-10)

But then, just when all seemed lost,

... the angel of the LORD called out to him from heaven, "Abraham! Abraham!"

"Here I am," he replied.

"Do not lay a hand on the boy," he said. "Do not do anything to him. Now I know that you fear God, because you have not withheld from me your son, your only son."

(v 11-12)

God provided a ram for the sacrifice instead. Isaac lived, and Abraham's descendants multiplied rapidly. One of those descendants, thousands of years later, was Jesus, and all who put their faith in him are adopted into his family, meaning Abraham's descendants really are too numerous to count.

Abraham was willing to sacrifice his own son in obedience to God because he was absolutely sure of what God had promised. The writer to the Hebrews says that "God had said to him, 'It is through Isaac that your offspring will be reckoned'" and therefore "Abraham reasoned that God could even raise the dead" (Hebrews 11 v 18-19). Abraham was so confident that God would do what he had promised through Isaac, that he was willing to obey, even when it looked crazy. His faith in the big picture meant that he was able to obey in the present; his faith in God's long-term plan meant that he surrendered in the short-term; he gave up the son he *could* see, on the assurance of a promise that he *couldn't* see. That's real faith.

Too often though, we want God to deliver in the short-term. We interpret the lesson of Abraham's life as "if you wait long enough, and do the right things, God will give you what you want". Singles are told, as I was by well-meaning friends, to "get themselves out there" more, to dress differently or fix their character flaws, and then God will reward them with a husband. Those with chronic illnesses are told to try this healing ministry or that therapy, they are challenged to repent more deeply or have more faith, and then God will heal them. It's a natural impulse to want to encourage those facing challenges with the idea that God will give them the thing they are asking him for, but we rarely ask for the real treasures he promises. We have available to us "the riches of his glorious inheritance … and his incomparably great power" (Ephesians 1 v 18-19). We could be filled with eternal pleasures that start now and continue for ever (Psalm 16 v 11), but instead we ask for temporal, ephemeral things that will quickly pass away (1 Corinthians 7 v 29-31).

In her outstanding book, *Born Again This Way*, Rachel Gilson shares the story of her friend Emily. Emily grew up in a non-Christian home, and from puberty experienced exclusively same-sex attractions. After becoming a Christian as a young adult, Emily began to wrestle with what her new identity in Christ meant for her. She describes coming to the realisation that she would no longer be able to have romantic relationships with women: "Walking home, with tears streaking down my face, I realized both that I could spend my entire life single as a result of that fact and that it would still be worth it. I said to myself, 'I love Jesus more'" (*Born Again This Way*, p 135).

As we wrestle for contentment, we know that every trial has come "so that the proven genuineness of your faith—

of greater worth than gold, which perishes even though refined by fire—may result in praise, glory and honour when Jesus Christ is revealed" (1 Peter 1 v 7). Until then, the road of obedience to Christ is not an easy one. And yet the glorious promise of Jesus is not just for the future. Even today, when we choose to fix our eyes on Jesus, to gaze on God's glory, to be more consumed by it than by our wants and needs, we will be filled and deeply satisfied (see Luke 1 v 53); and we will find ourselves "being transformed into his image with ever-increasing glory" (2 Corinthians 3 v 18).

SO, "WHO KILLS PRINCE HUMPERDINCK?"

Remember the *Princess Bride* story? Back in my babysitting days, I used to occasionally introduce the girls I looked after to new films. Sometimes they would have the same kind of response as the grandson in that film—at the point of the story where all seemed lost, they would turn to me with anxious eyes and ask how it would turn out. "But do they get together?" "Does she manage to escape?" *Will there be a happy ending?*

Rather than revealing the answers, I would ask them questions: "Do you think I would show you a film that had a bad ending? Have I ever shown you one that didn't work out before?" I was asking them to trust me. Based on what they knew of my character and our relationship, based on past experience, could they trust that it would be ok this time?

Are you wondering how things in your life could ever become right? Are you doubting that God could ever turn your situation around so that this setback or sickness, disappointment or delay could possibly be used for good? Are you struggling to understand his work (or apparent lack of it) in your life? Claire talked, in her story at the beginning of this chapter, about having an attitude of thankfulness. Think back over the ways that God has blessed and strengthened you in the past, and take time to thank him. Tell yourself truths about who you are in him, what he has done for you, and what he has promised you—look up some of the verses quoted in this chapter if that helps.

And when you're looking for evidence of God's character, don't just look at your own life. Look to the Scriptures. There we have the testimony of "a great cloud of witnesses" (Hebrew 12 v 1) telling us that he is faithful and trustworthy and loving and good. We have his promises in black and white, sealed with Jesus' blood. We have his declaration that "it is finished" (John 19 v 30), that "death has been swallowed up in victory" (1 Corinthians 15 v 54). And so, trusting in who we know him to be, "we fix our eyes not on what is seen, but on what is unseen, since what is seen is temporary, but what is unseen is eternal" (2 Corinthians 4 v 18), and it is totally worth it.

Ruth's story
Memorials of faithfulness

Greg and I got married when I was 20 and he was 21. He had 50 pence in the bank at the time. I had the deposit for a house. By the age of 25 I was living in my dream home, we had settled down, and I was ready to have babies. Then Greg dropped it onto me that he felt called to full-time ministry. He'd felt the call since he was sixteen, but had never thought to tell me. We can laugh about it now—but at the time I was shocked and upset. If you can imagine a dog, sat on its backside, being dragged along, that was me coming into ministry. I did not want this, and God had to really work on me.

One of the things I resented most was the fact that we had to sell our dream home, leave all my family and friends in the north of England and move down south to live in the manse that came with my husband's new job. It was hard living in a manse. We lived right next door to the church, so we'd have people looking through the window and saying, "New kitchen curtains? How did you afford those? I haven't got new kitchen curtains!" or "You've got a microwave?! Where did that come from?" Seriously. It wasn't easy.

I remember talking to a lady one day who told me, "Don't be so ungrateful; you've got a lovely roof over your head". And yes, I did, but in my longing for what I had "lost", all I could think was, "You live in your own home, and you don't understand what it feels like". And God spoke to me through his word, saying, "Godliness with contentment is great gain" (1 Timothy 6 v 6).

God had me on a journey of learning to trust him in all circumstances. I had to come to a point where I could say, "Lord, I'm going to lay this down. I'm not going to hold onto it." Bricks and mortar had become my security. I had felt secure before when I'd had my own home. And God was teaching me, "No, your security has got to be in me". So I had to lay that down.

And God has been so gracious in his provision for us— Greg and I actually own three houses now! How did that ever happen? I never thought I would ever own my own home again; I had come to a point where that was ok with me. And now we have three.

All these lessons I had learned about being content in God and trusting him were again massively put to the test in the "*annus horribilis*" year when we lost five babies in our immediate family. Greg's twin sister lost twins at seven months, my brother lost a one-year-old child, my cousin, who I was very close to, had a baby born with half a heart, and he lived for five days. And then halfway through a pregnancy, at twenty weeks, I lost a child. That was a tough year.

At the end of that year, one of the church members said to me, "Ruth, it's been really horrible watching what you guys have gone through this year. But one thing I have seen throughout it all, is that 'underneath are the everlasting arms' (Deuteronomy 33 v 27). I've seen how God has kept you through this year." And that was true. That was our experience. Even when you are going through really tough times, God is there, he is faithful. That is my experience.

When the children of Israel went through the wilderness, they built piles of stones as reminders for themselves, so they could say to their children, *This is what God did in this place* (Joshua 4 v 1-24). That's what I want my story to be. My hope for my life is not to accumulate more bricks-and-mortar houses but to build a memorial of God's faithfulness as a reminder for myself and an encouragement for you. God has done these things for me. He'll do it for you. He's faithful.

Chapter 5

PRACTISING CONTENTMENT

Sometimes we imagine that spiritual virtues like contentment will simply waft down from the sky and land on us while we're not watching. Or perhaps that they're like spiritual gifts, where some of us are given one and others receive another. Paul says otherwise. As we've already seen, he says the secret of contentment is something we can learn:

I have learned to be content whatever the circumstances. I know what it is to be in need, and I know what it is to have plenty. I have <u>learned</u> the secret of being content in any and every situation, whether well fed or hungry, whether living in plenty or in want.

(Philippians 4 v 11-12, my emphasis)

So far, we've wrestled with the truths that God is good, that he is sufficient to meet all our needs, and that the end of the story that he is writing will be infinitely worth anything we suffer in the present. But how do we take all that and pursue contentment day to day? How do we put those truths into practice in the midst of life's little annoyances and big longings?

CHOOSE IT

When I give talks on this, I ask for a few volunteers at the beginning of the talk, and have them pick out two pieces of fruit from a selection of apples, pears, bananas and oranges. Then I tell them they're not allowed to eat the fruit, but must hold onto it throughout the talk. They return to their places, and before long I ask everyone to take out their Bibles and turn to the reading. Sometimes people are able to juggle their fruits to hold them in one hand, others have to ask their neighbours for help, others just don't bother trying.

I explain that the fruit represents the things we're asking God for—the dreams we're holding onto, thinking we need them in order to be fully satisfied in life. They may be good things—that's why I use fruit instead of chocolate bars or gooey cream cakes. There's nothing wrong with wanting marriage, children, health, a better job, more security, a safer place to live—these are all blessings from God that can enrich our lives and extend his kingdom. We can be asking for good things with good motivations, but if we've reached the point where the desire for them is making us discontent, we need to make a choice. Do we keep holding onto that desire, or do we daily seek to let it go, so that we can take hold of him and enjoy the contentment he offers?

If we choose to hold onto the things we lack or the things we have lost, we're effectively choosing frustration, anger, disappointment with God and ultimately deep bitterness. This bitterness, this seed of distrust of God, will spread through our lives like rot through an apple. It will corrode our love, our hope, our joy, our security—not just in God but in every area of life. It will shrivel our faith, damage our health and cripple our relationships. We have all met people who carry a cloud of bitterness and unforgiveness around with them—and it's not pretty. As Sheridan Voysey says, "Perhaps a greater tragedy than a broken dream is a life forever defined by it" (*Resurrection Year*, p xii).

PRACTISE GRATITUDE

In Philippians 4 v 4 Paul commands us: "Rejoice in the Lord always. I will say it again: rejoice!"

This isn't something that comes naturally to us—otherwise he wouldn't have to tell us to do it—it's a choice. The fact that he *does* command us to do it shows that we have more power over our brains than we think.

I learned that when I was dieting once. If I went to work in the morning without planning what I would have for dinner, then by the time I came home, tired and hungry, all I could think of was greasy, fatty food. All I could imagine wanting was some quick, microwave ready meal, so that's what I'd have. If, however, before I left for work, I took a chicken breast or piece of salmon out of the freezer to defrost, and checked to make sure I had some nice, colourful mixed veg to go with it, then on the way home, that's what I'd be looking forward to eating. I'd have a mental image of a bright, attractive plate of tasty, healthy food, that would take minutes to cook, and that's what I would eat.

I could let my brain run where it wanted, and live as a victim of its bad choices. Or I could train it to focus on what I wanted it to, and live in the freedom of the good choices it now had available to it. It's no different with gratitude. Either I can live as a victim of my circumstances, or of the weather, or of the mood I wake up in each morning, or I can choose to be thankful to God for all he is and all he has done—and rejoice.

One of my favourite stories about this comes from *The Hiding Place*, Corrie ten Boom's classic autobiography. During World War II, Corrie was imprisoned with her sister, Betsie, in a Nazi concentration camp, for helping Jews to escape from occupied Holland. They were assigned to a dormitory that was smelly, dark, cramped and, worst of all, swarming with fleas. Betsie reminded her despairing sister of the Bible passage they had read that morning: "Rejoice always, pray continually, give thanks in all circumstances; for this is God's will for you in Christ Jesus" (1 Thessalonians 5 v 16-18).

The sisters looked for things to give thanks for—that they were together; that they had managed to smuggle their Bible in; that the overcrowded conditions meant more women to share the gospel with. When it came to the fleas, though, Corrie drew the line: "There's no way even God can make me grateful for a flea."

The sisters began to hold secret worship services in their dormitory at night. As the group studying and praying together grew, they were mystified as to why the guards didn't interfere. Then one afternoon, someone in the dormitory had a question about the work she was supposed to be doing, but the supervisor refused to come in and sort it out. "She wouldn't step through the door and neither would the guards," Betsie told Corrie later. "And you know why? ... Because of the fleas! That's what she said, 'That place is crawling with fleas!'" (*The Hiding Place*, p 185, 194-195)

Betsie's daily choice to practise thankfulness, mixed with her utter reliance on God and belief in his goodness, gave her a joyful contentment that radiates through the pages of this remarkable book. If you've never read it, I really recommend that you do (and if you have—read it again!).

Most of us have far more to be thankful for than two middle-aged sisters in a concentration camp. Yet we often find it just as hard as Corrie did to think of things to praise God for. The less we thank him for, however, the wider we open the door of our hearts for discontentment to seep in.

One way we practise gratitude is by talking to ourselves. It's not a mark of insanity, but a powerful way of training our brains. When you were learning times tables, or French verb forms, or Shakespeare quotes for your English

Literature exam, you practised by saying them—often out loud—over and over again. "One two is two, two twos are four ...", "*Je suis, tu es, il est, elle est...*", "O time, thou must untangle this, not I. / It is too hard a knot for me t'untie" (*Twelfth Night*, Act 2 Scene 2).

Now, you don't need to go around chanting mantras to yourself (although that might be helpful), but learn how to "take every thought captive" (2 Corinthians 10 v 5, ESV) and counter the negative, doubting, discontented ones with truth. The 20th-century preacher Martyn Lloyd-Jones said, "Have you realised that most of your unhappiness in life is due to the fact that you are listening to yourself instead of talking to yourself?"

Our tendency is to let our minds run where they want with a constant stream of thoughts. But Lloyd-Jones points out that the psalmist's response, in Psalm 42 v 5, was to talk back, to refuse to allow his "self" to dictate his thought life:

"Why are you cast down, O my soul?" he asks. His soul had been depressing him, crushing him. So he stands up and says: "Self, listen for a moment, I will speak to you." (*Spiritual Depression*, p 20-21)

The psalmist twice tells his soul to "put your hope in God" and declares in faith, "for I will yet praise him, my Saviour and my God" (42 v 5, 11).

Shortly after writing this, I caught myself grumbling as I wove my way through London's crowded streets, and decided to practise what I'd been preaching. I thanked God for placing me in this amazing city. I thanked him for an era of quick and easy global travel and of prosperity, peace and safety. In April 2020, I walked those same streets again, with barely another soul in sight. One microscopic virus had spread across the world and driven whole nations into lockdown. The things we take for granted can be snatched away more easily than we could imagine. But God is eternal, and always worthy to be praised.

So start today. Talk to God and tell him what you're thankful for. Or write a list, and don't stop until the page is full—include not just material blessings, but all that God has done for you and given to you and promised to you in Christ. Find a few of your favourite, faith-building verses that remind you of God's grace to you and try to memorise them (if you don't know where to start, try Psalm 42, or some of the verses I listed in chapter 1). Repeat them to yourself as you make a cup of coffee or walk along the street. And when your mind goes to that thing you don't have—when you feel that tide of discontent rising as you scroll through Instagram or watch the other parents at the school gate—choose to "rejoice in the Lord" instead.

LEARN TO LAMENT

I don't mean we should simply brush our desires, needs and dreams under the carpet. The goal is not to pretend that this ache in our souls doesn't hurt, or to squash it down and suppress it. Instead, we need to bring that pain before God. There is nothing sinful in saying, "Lord, this hurts", or even in pleading with him to change our circumstances. This is what the Bible calls lament. Psalm 13 is a wonderful model of this:

How long, LORD? Will you forget me for ever?
How long will you hide your face from me?
How long must I wrestle with my thoughts
and day after day have sorrow in my heart?
How long will my enemy triumph over me?
Look on me and answer, LORD my God.
Give light to my eyes, or I will sleep in death,
and my enemy will say, 'I have overcome him,'
and my foes will rejoice when I fall.
But I trust in your unfailing love;
my heart rejoices in your salvation.
I will sing the LORD's praise,
for he has been good to me.

There is no indication that the psalmist has received the answers or help he is asking for, yet in verses 5-6 he chooses to remind himself of the truth he believes about God: "I trust in your unfailing love; my heart rejoices in your salvation. I *will* sing the LORD's praise, for *he has been good to me*" (my emphasis). In the words of the author Andrew Wilson: "After a period of weeping, the believer begins worshipping God in the darkness" (*The Life You Never Expected*, p 24-25).

Have you ever really allowed yourself to lament over the thing that is robbing you of joyful contentment? It might feel silly to cry over it, particularly if it's something you know isn't that significant in the grand scheme of things.

But simply pushing it down and pretending it isn't painful won't help in the long run, nor will churning it over and over in your mind. Take it to God and have an honest conversation with him about how you're feeling.

A friend once asked me, "Do you think it's ok to pray about something like this?" My answer was a resounding "YES!"— and it is to you, too. God knows what you're thinking and feeling; you might as well talk to him about it!

Start with the psalm above, if you don't know how to go about it. Write out the first two verses, then write down what the issue is—let all the emotions out onto the page. Then, when you are ready, write out the second section— asking God to help you. Be specific. Then finally, the third section. If you can't pray it honestly yet, ask God to help you to trust him, to rejoice in his salvation, and to remember his goodness to you.

COPY OTHERS

When people are struggling with contentment, or unanswered prayers, or obedience to God's will, or a range of associated topics, they tend to either dig into the Christian community, or duck out. And among those who duck out, who isolate themselves "just for a season" while they deal with whatever the issue is, the chances of them returning seem to diminish with every missed Sunday, every avoided Bible study, every skipped prayer meeting. If you want to work through whatever you're struggling with, stay connected to your church family.

While Sheridan and Merryn Voysey were going through their journey of childlessness, they were part of a small group that met on Friday nights for food, Bible study and prayer. "We liked, loved, and listened to each other," Sheridan shares, "seeking Jesus together through life's joys and trials. There were times when Merryn and I could no longer pray, and these Friday night friends filled the gap. Like the four men in the Gospel story who lowered their paralytic friend through the roof to Jesus, this little group brought us to God when all we could do was lie motionless" (*Resurrection Year*, p 169).

So dig in to your Christian friendships—and use technology to help you. My church runs on WhatsApp groups. Ok, the notifications can be overwhelming at times. But I have been struck by the strong correlation between lack of engagement on our small group WhatsApp chat from some members and their ongoing struggles. And if you're in a situation which prevents you from physically meeting with other Christians, technology can be a real lifeline. There's nothing magic about sending a WhatsApp message to a group or participating in a Zoom call—it won't heal you/change your circumstances/bring resolution to your problems. But it does have a way of binding hearts together and stimulating prayer and practical support.

Now, it might be that you long for this kind of community. Perhaps you've turned to your church or small group for support and have been let down. Multiple times. I'm sorry. I think this is an area for real repentance for many churches in the west. It is a sign that we are not taking seriously the fact of our unity in Christ. As the author Sam Allberry puts it, drawing from Romans 12 v 4-5, "We're a body. *We belong to one another.* What happens to part of us therefore affects all. If some struggle, it hurts us all. *We're invested in one another*" (*7 Myths About Singleness*, p 15, my emphasis). This is not an aspiration or a nice goal to aim for. It is a truth. A statement of fact: we *are* the body of Christ. So if your church has wronged you, it is legitimate for you to feel hurt and disappointed. But we must forgive, and we must keep trying. Their sanctification is at stake as well as our well-being.

If you bruise your foot, the solution is not to cut it off and put it in a quiet room to heal. It won't. It will get much worse, very, very quickly! It has to stay connected to the body, no matter how painful or inconvenient that is for it or all the other parts. Only in union with the body can broken limbs and bruised organs really heal—and the whole body grow in health and strength.

There's another reason that Christian community is so important. It's not just that our friends comfort and support us on the journey—they teach us, too. In Philippians 4 v 9 Paul says, "Whatever you have learned or received or heard from me, or seen in me—put it into practice". He was telling the believers in Philippi to learn *from him*, to follow his example, to copy the things he did. That might come across as very arrogant, particularly in our day and age where we are increasingly distrustful of "experts" and authority figures. Or maybe it's just that we have different sources of authority. If we need information, we type a question into our favourite search engine, or ask our phones or the little black box in the corner of the room. If we want to improve ourselves, we buy a "self-help" book. But a self-help book can't answer your questions if you don't understand something, or help you apply it to your particular circumstances. Alexa can't hold you accountable or follow up to see how you're doing. Wikipedia can't lead by example. But God has placed us in churches with a whole load of people who can.

I've learned a lot about how to wrestle for contentment from watching one of my friends. She is married to a Christian man, but for a long time he wasn't quite the leader in their family that she had hoped for. And as she grew in spiritual maturity, he seemed to stagnate, getting left behind rather than leading her deeper. He was a good provider and a faithful husband, but she was discontented, longing for more.

Over several years I watched as she wrestled with God, continuing to grow in her own faith, daily choosing to praise God, serve him with all her heart and remain faithful to her husband. She never spoke ill of him in public, never moaned about how she wished he would help more with the kids, never sniped at him in front of others. She modelled love and respect, and behind the scenes, encouraged by one or two trusted friends, she prayed for him, and for more of God's love and patience. Over time he has become a more active father, taking an interest in the children when they're around, and initiating conversations, games and activities with them. And alongside that, my friend has become more contented as she seeks to walk closely with the Lord. She tells me, "Contentment came as a result of learning that God is in control and is infinitely more good, more loving than I ever imagined. I learned to trust him with my husband instead of trying to control or fight the situation."

Who are the more mature believers around you—the people whose character you admire in certain areas? Learn from them. Watch them, listen to them, hang out with them if you can, and learn their secrets. Ask them how they've struggled for contentment in the past, and how they've overcome it.

And who do you see good fruits starting to grow in that you can encourage? Community isn't all about our own growth and development—in fact, it's more about looking to help others grow and develop. We see in Paul not just joyful contentment but a passion for the gospel, a concern for others, and a commitment to discipling and encouraging everyone. And it seems that this was part of his secret of contentment: when we're focusing on the needs of others we find far greater joy, meaning and purpose than when we're looking at ourselves.

What we have seen in Paul, then, let us put into practice.

LOOK TO GOD MORE THAN THE THING YOU LONG FOR

Ultimately, though, the only person who is going to meet our deepest need and give us the joyful contentment we long for is Jesus. As one old hymn puts it:

Turn your eyes upon Jesus,
Look full in His wonderful face,
And the things of earth will grow strangely dim,
In the light of His glory and grace.
(*Turn Your Eyes Upon Jesus*, Helen Howarth Lemmel)

Or in the words of the Victorian preacher Charles Spurgeon:

Would you lose your sorrows? Would you drown your cares? Then go, plunge yourself in the Godhead's deepest sea; be lost in his immensity; and you shall come forth as from a couch of rest, refreshed and invigorated. I know nothing which can so comfort the soul; so calm the swelling billows of grief and sorrow; so speak peace to the winds of trial, as a devout musing upon the subject of the Godhead.

(Quoted in Alistair Begg, *Pray Big*, p 60)

How do we lose ourselves in the immensity of God? It will look different from person to person. You may need to build up a stockpile of what Andrew and Rachel Wilson refer to as "emergency joy fuel"—things you can go to that you know will quickly help in times of need. These may include particular worship songs, favourite Psalms, or a book of short devotional thoughts. Maybe your awe and wonder at God increases as you wrestle with the meaning of obscure Greek words in Scripture; or as you walk in nature; or as you worship with a crowd of others or stand on a hilltop gazing up at the stars. If I have time, the surest way I've found to reset my equilibrium and refocus my mind and heart on God is to take my camera and a few favourite sermon downloads and explore a new area of London, marvelling at God's gift of creativity to artists and architects and letting truth about him seep into my mind.

These are, in a sense, crisis management tools, or the equivalent of a refreshing summer holiday. Yet while holidays are good and important, they should come as enhancements to, rather than replacements for, the day-to-day rhythms of nutrition, exercise and rest that help our bodies run smoothly.

The same principle holds true for our spiritual routines. Our injections of "emergency joy fuel" should be top-ups to a daily discipline of prayer and Bible reading, not our sole source of spiritual nutrition. Choosing to spend even a short time each day reading the Scriptures and praying for yourself and others will, over time, sink your roots deep and grow a strong, resilient core to your faith.

A breakthrough in this came for me in 2015, when I received a small, slimline planner from a charity I support. Each week was spread over two pages, and each day had five short lines. I thought, "I could write five lines of prayer per day". So I tried it. Just five lines per day (which gradually increased to ten as my writing got smaller and smaller to fit in all I wanted to say). Each week was numbered, and one day I realised I was on about week 15 without even noticing, then week 21, then week 30. Things got a bit patchy in November and December, but for ten whole months I had prayed at least something almost every day. The following year I bought a slightly bigger planner and did it again, and again the year after. Over the next few years I started adding more Bible reading too. I don't think it's any coincidence that my contentment breakthrough came 18 months into my newfound discipline of prayer.

Before this, my prayers had mostly been the sporadic, self-focused prayers of desperation. Yet as I began to pray daily for others, lifting up their concerns as well as my own, my relationship with God deepened. Rather than viewing him as a Father who refused to give me what I wanted, I began to meet him as the One who cared about the needs of my friends and family. He in turn gave me a greater love for them. He lifted my gaze beyond my singleness, and as a result that issue was able to find its rightful place in my thinking and assume its real, much smaller, proportions.

The secret of being content isn't really all that secret, as it turns out. Many people over the centuries have learned it, and we can too as we make a choice to follow their example, practise gratitude, embrace community and daily fix our eyes on Jesus.

Tanya's story
Wrestling for answers

In the space of one day, my life changed. Before, I was living out my calling as a Bible teacher and lecturer in theology, happily married and awaiting my first baby with eager expectation. It was childbirth that changed everything.

I suffer from Myalgic Encephalomyelitis (M.E.), a serious neurological illness. It's like having a very low battery that never fully recharges and is accompanied with a side serving of pain, dizziness, digestive problems, cognitive dysfunction and heart problems. I was already in a wheelchair because of it, but going through labour broke my body further. Nine years on, I am still confined to bed 21 hours a day. To leave the house—for anything—I must save up my energy for two weeks. I need to be pushed in a wheelchair, have my meals provided, and often need help getting dressed.

In the early days, amidst the panic and confusion of attempting to raise a baby while being as helpless as him,

I railed against God. I loved my child, and reasoned that if I had the power to stop him being as ill and miserable as I was, I would do it in a heartbeat. If I was God's child, how could he be good when he didn't stop this?

It's a question I had previously explored rationally and had the right answers to, but now I felt it like a howl of pain. As I grieved the loss of my ministry, my independence, my freedom and my health, I had to walk through a long time of darkness and anger, wrestling with God for answers. For me, the thing that most helped was hearing a challenge by a speaker called Kay Warren, who lost her son to suicide in 2013: evil will come, because evil will come, because evil will come. Do we want to do it with or without God?

That's where I started, not from a position of having worked out the whys, but in walking with God, and assuming he was good, even though life was hard. Today, my theology acknowledges the parallel truths that God is good and powerful, and life is full of suffering, and I leave a lot of space for his Spirit to work in my heart in the gap between those truths.

I've had nine years to come to terms with my new life. Right now, if I'm honest, I'm in the middle of fresh grief about it. Those bursts of grief don't go away, but they do lessen.

As I've rebuilt my life, walking a long journey towards acceptance and contentment, I've benefitted from the honesty of others in suffering. And I've benefitted from the honesty of the Bible, through the characters that pour out their anger and objections to God, seeking God even as they don't understand it. We don't have to wait to feel content before we can approach God; neither do we need to beat ourselves up for not feeling content yet. These things take time, and God has time.

Another thing that's helped is realising that although my ministry is a different shape, I still have it. God opened up doors for writing, as my blog became more and more popular, and I realised I could still minister, even from my bed. It is a grace I do not take for granted. My book, *Those Who Wait*, is a creative exploration of four Bible characters who struggled with the frustration of waiting, and is written for people like me who want to find God in disappointment, doubt and delay.

Some days I feel content, on other days I weep; but I have found comfort, and can say today that life is hard and God is good—and I look to heaven as the true hope of contentment and comfort.

———

Tanya Marlow is the author of *Those Who Wait: Finding God in Disappointment, Doubt and Delay* (Malcolm Down, 2017). You can find more of her work at https://tanyamarlow.com.

Chapter 6

BURNING QUESTIONS

Our culture is not comfortable with ambiguity. I'm not sure any culture ever has been, but it is certainly true that in our internet age we expect clear and instant answers to everything. And if anything goes wrong, we assume that somebody somewhere must be responsible.

It's therefore not surprising that we can intellectually assent to all the ideas we've covered so far, but in a corner of our hearts still be crying out, "But why? Why can't this all be easier?" And for the deeper, darker valleys of life, "Why me? Why this? What did I do wrong?"

The easy answer, I'm afraid, is that there are no easy answers. Sorry. But here are some ways to think about the questions, to dig deeper into the doubts and fears that lie at their roots, and to deal with the issues they reveal.

WHAT DID I DO WRONG?
In Psalm 84 v 11, the psalmist declares that God withholds "no good thing" from those whose way of life is blameless.

It is possible to hear that as a criticism or condemnation: *he doesn't withhold good things from good people, therefore if he is withholding something good from me, it must mean I haven't been good enough.*

Let me be very clear: that is emphatically *not* what the Bible teaches.

That was the argument of Job's friends—*you must have sinned for God to be doing this to you*—and God told them in no uncertain terms that they were wrong and misrepresenting him.

It was the assumption of the disciples when they saw a blind man in John 9:

[Jesus'] disciples asked him, "Rabbi, who sinned, this man or his parents, that he was born blind?"

"Neither this man nor his parents sinned," said Jesus, "but this happened so that the works of God might be displayed in him." (v 1-3)

If you are going through hard times, it is not because you are being punished for your sin. The New Testament teaching is that if you are a Christian, you have been declared blameless in God's sight. Once you have put your faith in Christ, the old, blame-ridden, sinful you has been put to death and you have risen with Christ as a new creation (2 Corinthians 5 v 17). Jesus has taken every ounce of punishment you deserve for your wrongdoing. So you are no longer that guilty person, but a completely new, clean, holy one, for ever. And this status is not something you have earned—it's something you're given. You are saved by God's grace (Ephesians 2 v 8-9). You didn't earn your way into salvation, and you can't earn your way out of it, either.

Now we have another dilemma, though. If God doesn't withhold good things from his children, and he is withholding a good thing you've been asking for, how do we resolve that? After all, Jesus told us:

Which of you, if your son asks for bread, will give him a stone? Or if he asks for a fish, will give him a snake? If you, then, though you are evil, know how to give good gifts to your children, how much more will your Father in heaven give good gifts to those who ask him!

(Matthew 7 v 9-11)

We also know, though, that sometimes when a child asks for bread, we give them fruit instead. Bread is good, but a diet of only bread will not give them the nutrients they need. So a good parent doesn't always give their child what they ask for. Sometimes we may give them nothing, because we know that dinner time is approaching, and we want to give them a full meal then.

This can be hard. Andrew Wilson, in an analogy he got from his friend Ann Blaber, compares it to being given a real orange for dessert when everyone else at the party is tapping open chocolate oranges (*The Life You Never Expected*, p 33-35. If you live in a part of the world without chocolate oranges, they are exactly what they sound like: chocolate that's shaped like and tastes like an orange!). We might know it is objectively better to have a real orange, but that doesn't stop us feeling jealous or left out. So we have to wrestle once again with our big questions:

Is God good? It doesn't feel like it, because he hasn't given me what I wanted... but, in the words of a former mentor of mine, "I know that I know that I know that he is", so I am going to choose to believe that.

Is God enough? I think I need a chocolate orange to "hit the spot" and satisfy the hunger that I'm feeling, but God has given me a real orange, or no orange, instead. Do I trust that "God will meet all [my] needs according to the riches of his glory in Christ Jesus" (Philippians 4 v 19)? I have to choose to believe that God will meet all my needs, and if he is not giving me the thing I yearn for, it must not be the thing I really need.

Is God worth it? Do I believe that he is worth more than any chocolate orange? Do I believe his promise that he is preparing for me a heavenly banquet, of not just chocolate oranges, but of food and drink that is beyond my imagination? Can I choose to give up the opportunity to eat chocolate now for his sake, believing that it is going to be worth it?

At the end of the day, we have to trust God when he says that the real orange is not a punishment but his best plan for us (keep reading for more on that). *"I will never stop doing good to [my people],"* he promises, "and I will inspire them to fear me, so that they will never turn away from me. *I will rejoice in doing them good* and will *assuredly* plant them in this land with all my heart and soul" (Jeremiah 32 v 40-41, my emphasis). He who has promised is faithful, and we can trust him.

BUT I'VE DONE EVERYTHING RIGHT...

This is a similar objection to the one above, but its root is subtly yet significantly different. It reveals a "vending-machine-Jesus" attitude.

I remember talking to someone once who just couldn't get past this barrier. She desperately wanted to be married, and couldn't imagine that life would be bearable, let alone happy, without that happening. I tried to talk to her about God's goodness, his sufficiency and his worth, but she just kept circling back to this one point, "But I've done everything right". She wasn't saying she was perfect or sinless, simply that she'd done all those things you're told to do to experience God's blessing. She had been to church faithfully, she had always read her Bible, she had lived a moral life, she had responded in obedience when God had called her to another country. In fact, she had an amazing testimony of God's provision for her in many areas—but this one thing she lacked. And her interpretation of the lack was that she had played her part, and now it was time for God to play his. She had put in her money, now where was the chocolate bar?

When we have this level of despair and disappointment with God over an area of lack in our lives, it indicates that we probably have an idolatry issue. If we complain that we have done everything that God requires but he hasn't done x for us in return, we reveal that our goal was never God, but was always secretly x. We want the gift, not the Giver.

What is your heart's motivation for "doing everything right"? Is it the natural overflow of your love for him and your desire to glorify him in all you say and do? Or is it because you are seeking the good that will come to you if you obey him?

I think most of us fluctuate between the two. I'm sure that for most of my friend's life her motivation had been obedience for its own sake. It was only as she reflected on her area of discontentment that she started to see her good actions as a bargaining tool.

This is definitely a trap I fell into. I remember trying several times to work out what I was doing wrong, why God wasn't sending me a husband. I'd been to university—a classic place to meet your future spouse. That hadn't worked. I was, at that time, a missionary for a ministry which involved travelling to churches all around the world, meeting innumerable committed Christian men. And that hadn't worked. Maybe I needed to work on my prayer life? Perhaps if I studied the Bible more, or lost weight, or tidied my house...? I wasn't seeing any value in these things for their own sake but merely as means to an end by which God would bring me my husband.

Sometimes we even manage to make our pursuit of contentment into a bargaining tool of its own. We can read stories—there are some in this book—of people who have reached the point of surrender to God's will, only to then be given the thing they were longing for in the first place: the childless couple who have miraculously conceived; the person who surrendered her desire for a home, and now owns three. So we seek to "be content" or "learn our lesson" as quickly as we can, so that God can get on with it and deliver the good stuff. But again, this is "vending machine" thinking—if I press the right buttons and turn the right dials and enter the right coin in the slot, I will get what I want out of it.

We need to reset our thinking on what we deserve, and what it means to be blessed. When we're honest with ourselves, we know we haven't done *everything* right. We've done good things with bad motivations, or we've omitted to do all the good we could have done. We haven't loved the Lord our God with *all* our heart, *all* our soul or *all* our mind, and we haven't loved *all* our neighbours as ourselves. There is much room for improvement. And yet, despite all our failings, our loving, compassionate Father "has blessed us in the heavenly realms with every spiritual blessing in Christ" (Ephesians 1 v 3). We already have far more than we deserve.

WHY WOULD GOD MAKE ME WITH THESE DESIRES BUT NOT LET ME USE THEM?

All I ever wanted was to be a stay-at-home mum. (After I'd grown out of wanting to be a ballerina, or a jockey, or an actress.) I was always great with kids and was good at the homemaking and hospitality skills I associated with the wifely role, too. So when that role didn't materialise, I was left with a question: Why would God create me with all those gifts and skills and propensities, then prevent me from living out the life he had designed me for?

You know what I'm going to say, by now—that ultimately we should be finding our fulfilment in him, not in the exercising of our gifts or in any position, role or relationship other than that of beloved child of God. But that still doesn't answer the "why". Why would he give us desires, gifts or abilities then withhold the opportunity to fulfil or use them?

Paul, in his letter to the Christians in Rome, reminds us that we are the equivalent of lumps of clay in the hands of a master potter—God (Romans 9 v 20-21). He has the right to make us in any form he chooses, then use us for his purposes, whatever they may be. For a long time I thought I knew better than God. I thought I knew how my gifts could be most useful to him. How arrogant!

Paul uses the pottery metaphor again in 2 Corinthians 4. He says we are like clay pots—ordinary, everyday objects—so that people don't praise us, but look past us to see God's glorious power (v 6-7). Maybe if God had let me use my gifts in the way I wanted, I would have got all the "glory". I wanted people to see what a great wife and mother I could be. When God withheld the fulfillment of that dream, it was a real blow to my pride. I had to come to the point where I was willing to lay down my dream and say, "Lord, I want to serve you and give you glory. I don't know why you would give me these gifts and not want to use them, but I choose to trust that your way is best. Help me to accept your will. And please use me in your way and in your timing."

Are you at a point where you could pray something like that? Why do you want that bigger house, that work promotion, that spouse? If it's to meet your own needs and desires, you may need to lay those down before the Lord. If it's because you want an extra bedroom so that you can foster needy children, or more money so that you can support world missions, or a marriage partnership so you can better serve your neighbours, perhaps God wants to fulfil those desires in other ways. We can be so focused on the method we have in mind, that we miss the opportunities right in front of us.

Maybe you need to pause right now and consider your "why". Then, if you are convicted that your motivation is wrong, ask God to forgive you. Or if you believe your motivation is right, ask him to help you trust him for the how and when.

There's another reason why God sometimes holds back on using us how we think he should. Have you ever noticed how easy it is to stop praying and relying on him when everything is going well? When we have all we want, and are living fulfilled, happy lives, we tend to think it's all down to our abilities and talents. We may occasionally remember to thank him for making us such a gifted wife/parent/Bible teacher or whatever, but it's all too easy to forget that we're totally reliant on him for everything. Could it be that sometimes he withholds things from us in order to remind us of our dependence on him? Maybe he is withholding that thing from you so that he can do things through you that show his power in your weakness (2 Corinthians 12 v 9).

If that seems like a waste of your talents, take another look at the apostle Paul. He was a very gifted preacher and evangelist—why would God gift him like that, and then imprison him, preventing him from travelling to different churches and unreached areas? Could it be because if Paul was busy doing all of that, we wouldn't have most of the New Testament? The teaching we have been learning from in this book, to the church in Philippi, would have been delivered to them first hand, and neither we nor any of the millions of churches down the centuries would have had the benefit. By restricting Paul's travel to a finite number of churches in his lifetime, God enabled him to minister to an almost infinite number for millennia. Not to mention the fact that all that deep, deep teaching was learned through his trials in the first place. God's economy is different to ours. What you see as a waste, God can use as a mighty blessing.

Or here's a more current example. There has been lots of excellent thinking and writing emerging in recent years on the church as community—books on hospitality and singleness and God's love for the outsider. And much of that thinking has come from Christians who are same-sex attracted, but are convinced that God requires them to say "no" to those desires. They have produced some fantastic materials, rich in theology and overflowing with love and compassion. (For starters, try Rachel Gilson's *Born Again This Way*, Rosaria Champagne Butterfield's *The Secret Thoughts of an Unlikely Convert* and *The Gospel Comes with a House Key*, Sam Allberry's *Why Does God Care Who I Sleep With?* and *7 Myths About Singleness*, and David Bennett's *A War of Loves*.)

Why is it coming from them? Because they have had to wrestle with what it means to obey God when our culture screams that sexual fulfilment is both a human right and an innate need, without which it is impossible to thrive (and, some seem to think, even to survive). The challenges they face have forced them to do the deep work, and to present truths about God to his church with a richness and nuance that may have been missing if it hadn't been for their struggle.

WHY ME?

So how come I "get" to be the one who has all this "blessing" and depth while my friends are free to eat all the chocolate oranges they want? It doesn't feel fair. And while I may objectively understand that it is for my long-term good, it is hard to take the short-term pain, especially when it feels like I'm the only one struggling.

First, we need to speak truth to ourselves—it is not just us. Look at the number of support groups, 12-step programmes and self-help books there are out there. Almost every Christian you know is struggling with something. Everyone is in pain or has some area of their life where they wish God would move. It's not just you—so why *not* you?

Second, as Job asked his wife, "Shall we accept good from God, and not trouble?" (Job 2 v 10). If God is God, if he is really Lord of our lives, if he is sovereign, does that not give him the right to allow us to face trials and sufferings as well as joys and pleasures? Yes, if he is good he will not cause his children arbitrary suffering, but what if our pain serves a greater purpose? Many Christians, when going through trials, have trained themselves to ask not, "Why me?" but, "What might God be doing here? How might he be wanting to use my pain for his glory?"

Scripture suggests that God could be doing at least three things through your pain.

First, he might be equipping you to comfort others. Paul writes that God "comforts us in all our troubles, so that we can comfort those in any trouble with the comfort we ourselves receive from God" (2 Corinthians 1 v 4).

When we're in difficult circumstances—or even just feeling the challenge of drowning in deadlines or being strangled by envy—one of the biggest challenges is the sense of isolation. We feel alone in the struggle, convinced that no one has ever encountered this before, worried that we're weird and that there's no hope of normality being restored.

There are two very powerful words that can make a big difference in these times: me too.

Feeling seen and understood can make all the difference. And God could be using this season in your life to shape you into the person who can say those words to others in theirs. As I have opened up about my struggles with friends at church, I have really seen God use it as a catalyst to help others find the courage to say, "I'm struggling, too. Can we talk?" When God uses you to help someone else find the way forward through their difficulties or discontentments, it is incredibly fulfilling. Maybe God is allowing you to experience this pain in order to use you as a source of life for others.

Second, God might be using your struggles to make you more like Christ. The goal of the Christian life is not to be comfortable or to be successful or to be blessed with all material and relational blessings; it is to be holy (Matthew 5 v 48; 1 Peter 1 v 16). It is to become more like Christ and to glorify God.

I don't know about you, but I'm not perfectly Christlike yet. There's a lot of refining still to be done, and that may well come through times of great trial. James tells me how to react when those times come: "Count it all joy ... for you know that the testing of your faith produces steadfastness. And let steadfastness have its full effect, that you may be perfect and complete, lacking in nothing" (James 1 v 2-4, ESV).

What kind of person do you want to be? Flaky and unreliable? Unstable and easily swayed? Weak and needy? Or do you want to be reliable and dependable, secure and contented, strong and steadfast? The latter is only achieved by persevering through difficulties. No one ever ran a marathon, wrote a bestseller or made a scientific breakthrough without going through lots of difficulties and setbacks along the way.

And part of what gave them the motivation to get there was seeing what was possible. This is another reason why we need to be in a place where we can learn from others. Look at the lives of Christlike people around you, read biographies of heroes of the faith, learn about what characteristics and attitudes God commends in the Bible—and of course set your eyes on Christ himself.

Therefore, since we are surrounded by such a great cloud of witnesses, let us throw off everything that hinders and the sin that so easily entangles. And let us run with perseverance the race marked out for us, fixing our eyes on Jesus, the pioneer and perfecter of faith. For the joy that was set before him he endured the cross, scorning its shame, and sat down at the right hand of the throne of God. Consider him who endured such opposition from sinners, so that you will not grow weary and lose heart.
(Hebrews 12 v 1-3)

God has ordained our circumstances like a customised personal training regime to get us through the marathon. So "endure hardship as discipline ... No discipline seems pleasant at the time, but painful. Later on, however, it produces a harvest of righteousness and peace for those who have been trained by it" (12 v 7, 11). Sometimes heaven is silent, sometimes our requests are not granted, because God wants to do something far bigger and better—to give us a deeper understanding of him and a strength that we never thought possible.

Third, our hardships can and will be used by God to advance the gospel. That's what Paul found with his imprisonment:

Now I want you to know, brothers and sisters, that what has happened to me has actually served to advance the gospel. As a result, it has become clear throughout the whole palace guard and to everyone else that I am in chains for Christ. And because of my chains, most of the brothers and sisters have become confident in the Lord and dare all the more to proclaim the gospel without fear.
(Philippians 1 v 12-14)

Notice the dual level of gospel witness that Paul mentions— the palace guard are hearing the gospel from Paul, but also, somehow, the other Christians in the city are gaining strength from Paul's imprisonment. That seems like a very unexpected consequence. In his second letter to Timothy, Paul seems to say that many Christians were ashamed of his imprisonment (2 Timothy 1 v 8, 15-17), but here the believers were actually emboldened. I'm sure it can't have been by the fact of his imprisonment—they weren't some kind of sadistic pain-seekers thinking, "If we share the gospel, maybe we'll get to be punished, too!" But they saw from Paul's example and attitude that being shut in a Roman jail wasn't the worst thing that could happen to them. Being unfruitful for God was worse by far. A quiet, comfortable life wasn't the best thing on offer—seeing the gospel bring life to others was far more exciting! That mission produced a fruit of joyful contentment in Paul that was better than a whole pile of chocolate oranges. Could God be using your experiences to open up doors for sharing how faithful he is even when life isn't all you thought it would be?

Those are three of the Bible's answers to the question, "Why me?" And they are far better than the alternatives: "Because God wants you to suffer", "Because he is powerless to prevent it" or "Because he's just mean and capricious and you drew the short straw today". If those are the things your heart is telling you, stop right here and take those fears and objections to God. Go to his word and look up what he says about you and about himself. If you don't know where to start, try Zephaniah 3 v 17, Psalm 145 v 8-9, Matthew 10 v 29-31, Jeremiah 31 v 3, or Psalm 139.

Don't believe the lies of the enemy; trust the words of your Father. Wrestle with these things and work through them until you are certain that God is good, he is all-powerful and he does love you, or you will never find the contentment you're longing for.

There are lots of things we don't know. But there are some things we do. When author Joni Eareckson Tada received her second cancer diagnosis in November 2018 she wrote:

I relaxed and smiled, knowing that my sovereign God loves me dearly and holds me tightly in his hands. What good is it if we only trust the Lord when we understand his ways? That only guarantees a life filled with doubts. (www.joniandfriends.org/joni-eareckson-tada-receives-new-cancer-diagnosis, accessed 17 Jan 20)

INCOMPREHENSIBLY MARVELLOUS

God never does things the way we expect—people who are fantastic speakers get confined to bed for 21 hours a day, people who would make wonderful parents are able neither to conceive nor to adopt, people who could have a fantastic ministry around the world are given two very needy children under their own roof. Even people who were saving the lives of hundreds of Jews are captured and put in concentration camps. We can't comprehend why God does what he does, but to try is as absurd as a piece of clay giving the potter advice about how to shape it and use it.

But when we see what he can do when we surrender our willing hearts, it causes us to marvel and to praise him for his wondrous works, which are far beyond our comprehension. Which brings us right back to where we started—to the "who" behind all our "whats".

*Oh, the depth of the riches of the wisdom and knowledge
of God!*

   How unsearchable his judgments,

   and his paths beyond tracing out!

"Who has known the mind of the Lord?

   Or who has been his counsellor?"

"Who has ever given to God,

   that God should repay them?"

For from him and through him and for him are all things.

   To him be the glory for ever! Amen. (Romans 11 v 33-36)

My story
Emptiness filled

In the spring of 2017, I realised that my prayers around my singleness had changed. I was no longer begging God to come through for me and give me a husband. Nor was I praying, as I had for a season, "Lord, I want your will… but if that could include a husband, I'd really appreciate it. Any time…"

I knew I'd still love to be married, but I also realised that God had given me a deep, satisfied, joyful contentment with where I was.

I shared this on the women's WhatsApp group at my church, wanting to give some hope to those at the beginning of this journey; those looking around in despair at the church with its imbalance of males to females (smaller than in non-London churches, but still significant); those who spent every summer weekend at hen parties/bridal showers or weddings, but with no hope of the same on their own horizons; those who were beginning to wonder if God could really be trusted with this area of their lives.

I got an incredible response. This affected far more people than I realised. I began to have opportunities to talk to some of them and pray with and for them. I'd love to be able to tell you that after one quick prayer, everyone found freedom from the fear and doubt and longing they felt. They didn't. It rarely works that quickly. I can look back to long sessions with a mentor in the early 2000s, the lessons from which are only just now beginning to make sense and bear fruit in my life. I could see the logic and the truth of them at the time, but I only really "got it" after years more of walking with God. He loves me. And that's all that matters. The sense of absolute security that this knowledge brings is a source of constant amazement to me. And as I've followed his lead through twists and turns, I've seen him open innumerable doors and lavishly provide for me. As the evidence of his faithfulness has stacked up in so many other areas, it has freed my heart to trust in and experience his goodness in this one.

So by 2017, having realised that I was actually loving his will for my life, and that he was good, enough and worth it, I was able to consciously surrender that desire for marriage.

It's amazing what a difference that has made across my life. I hadn't realised how much it had hindered me to be holding out for a husband. It was a good thing, but even carrying around something good restricts your hands from free movement. I've got a new level of joy and fruitfulness not just in my spiritual life but in my writing, in leadership, in hospitality, in discipling others in the church and in love for my neighbours outside it.

This desire that I thought was just a small, peripheral longing turned out to be a huge, idolatrous blockage that was affecting so many areas of my life.

As I've already said, my life's ambition was to be a stay-at-home mum. In one sense, it looks like God hasn't fulfilled that. Yet through my willingness to be open and vulnerable about my singleness, he has given me the opportunity to take on a "spiritual mothering" role in my church. I can meet with and pray for younger women (and some older ones), and he has given me a pastoral concern for them and a love for them which has been missing up till now. I am also partly self-employed (because of lots of work opportunities he has brought to me through many and varied connections), and work from home two or three days a week. That means I am able to cook for my life group each week, to reach out to lonely neighbours, to take in packages for half the street when they're out at work, and to be available during the day for students and shift workers who need more flexible times to come and chat.

I may not have a husband, but I'm doing almost all the things I thought I needed a husband to be able to do. Even my longing for physical intimacy no longer stings quite so deeply as I have grown in spiritual intimacy with God. I released the dreams I was clinging to, only to find that he gave them back in rich and wonderful ways I could never have imagined.

Conclusion
THE SECRET

So what was Paul's secret of being content? In one sense, he never quite spells it out. But as we read through Philippians, it's clear that it has something to do with the fact that he was more passionate about Christ and about the wellbeing of others than he was about his own needs. Nowhere is this dual passion seen more clearly than in Philippians 1 v 21-25:

For to me, to live is Christ and to die is gain. If I am to go on living in the body, this will mean fruitful labour for me. Yet what shall I choose? I do not know! I am torn between the two: I desire to depart and be with Christ, which is better by far; but it is more necessary for you that I remain in the body. Convinced of this, I know that I will remain, and I will continue with all of you for your progress and joy in the faith.

Paul says that he can't wait to die and be with Christ—that would be better to him than all the riches in the world. But then what would happen to the Philippians?

Getting his heart's desire would mean leaving the Christians in Philippi—and us—worse off without his teaching, and so Paul resolves to embrace life rather than longing for death.

This is perhaps an illustration of what it looks like to "Love the Lord your God with all your heart and with all your soul and with all your mind" and "Love your neighbour as yourself" (Matthew 22 v 37, 39). When we're passionately seeking to know Christ (Philippians 3 v 10), desiring that his gospel will be shared among the nations and that all believers would grow in maturity and godliness, that leaves very little time for worrying about our own needs and desires.

It is easy to be discontented when we're focusing on ourselves. The advertising industry relies on that fact, pointing our eyes to what we lack and telling us we won't be happy until we get it. The Facebook/Instagram empire makes a fortune by forcing us to constantly compare our lives with the carefully curated, artfully filtered lives of our friends, acquaintances and favourite celebrities. And sadly, many church sermons sell Jesus as a fix for our problems, rather than as the only hope for a hurting world.

It's much harder to be discontented when we focus on others—in compassion, not comparison. Betsie ten Boom illustrated this time and again in the concentration camp, when she rejoiced at overcrowding because it meant not more discomfort for her but more opportunities to share the gospel. Sheridan Voysey continues to discover it, as his suffering opens doors for him to minister to others and point them to the hope we have in Christ.

But it is absolutely impossible to be discontented when we focus on God's glory. That's something that the prophet Isaiah's vision of God enthroned in the temple shows us. We looked at it briefly in chapter 1, but it's worth looking at again in more detail:

> *In the year that King Uzziah died, I saw the Lord, high and exalted, seated on a throne; and the train of his robe filled the temple. Above him were seraphim, each with six wings: with two wings they covered their faces, with two they covered their feet, and with two they were flying. And they were calling to one another:*
>
> *"Holy, holy, holy is the LORD Almighty;*
> *the whole earth is full of his glory."*
>
> *At the sound of their voices the doorposts and thresholds shook and the temple was filled with smoke.*
>
> *"Woe to me!" I cried. "I am ruined! For I am a man of unclean lips, and I live among a people of unclean lips, and my eyes have seen the King, the LORD Almighty."*
> *(Isaiah 6 v 1-5)*

Was Isaiah waiting for the noise and smoke to die down so he could bring up that request for a bigger kitchen or a better job? No—in the face of God's majestic holiness, the only thing on Isaiah's mind was his own sinfulness and his need for mercy. All he wanted was to be made clean. His thoughts were not on having his earthly needs met but only on having his spiritual needs met—on being fit to stand in God's presence and worship him.

And those are needs that God graciously loves to meet: "Then one of the seraphim flew to me with a live coal in his hand, which he had taken with tongs from the altar. With it he touched my mouth and said, 'See, this has touched your lips; your guilt is taken away and your sin atoned for'" (Isaiah 6 v 6-7). It's a beautiful foreshadowing of what Christ's once-for-all sacrifice on the cross did for all his people: our guilt is taken away and our sin is atoned for.

And we see just a couple of verses later that this doesn't lead to complacency or apathy—it leads to action: "Then [Isaiah] heard the voice of the Lord saying, 'Whom shall I send? And who will go for us?' And [he] said, 'Here am I. Send me!'" (v 8). The bigger our view of God, the more we find our commitment to his will growing. As we cease being consumed by our own wants and needs, we find ourselves beginning to care about what is on God's heart. Whether that's a concern for justice, a passion for evangelism or a heart for discipleship (or some combination of the three), we find ourselves eagerly volunteering, compelled to do the work of God in the world. And that is when we discover that he is wonderfully able to use our lack for his glory. The very area of sin that Isaiah identified became the area that God redeemed for his own glory—the man of "unclean lips" became a man who spoke the words of God to Israel. When my love for God and *his* will grew greater than my desire for *my* will, my singleness was freed up to become a gift to him, the church and my neighbours, and I found the joyful contentment I had thought could only be provided by a husband.

There's nothing wrong with asking for the thing you want—Jesus did that in Gethsemane ("My Father, if it is possible, may this cup be taken from me", Matthew 26 v 39). So to become Christlike is not to stop desiring, hoping, longing or feeling, but it is to desire, hope for, long for and feel passionate about our Father's will more than our own ("Yet not as I will, but as you will"). It is to open our hands, release the dream we have been clinging onto so tightly, and cling to him instead.

Yes, this can be painful. Yes, it is hard to keep being disappointed month after month, or to face challenge after challenge. God gives us these circumstances as opportunities to grow in Christlikeness, but when they've gone on so long, so relentlessly, and we're tired and weary in body, mind and spirit, it is natural to want to give up. "I don't want to grow any more," we sigh. "I don't want to be pruned, no matter how loving the gardener. I don't want to go through the refiner's fire again. I'm happy being a straggly plant or a low-grade bar of gold." Except of course, that we're not happy there. If you've read this book, my guess is that you're discontent with life as it is, or are struggling to cope with the things it has thrown at you. Maybe this path of pruning or refinement is the one that will lead you to the peace and joy you've been longing for.

We tend to put ourselves in the centre of our stories. If you're the main character in the movie of your life, then you expect that eventually things will work out the way you wanted them. You'll get the guy/girl, the miracle will happen, the healing will come... the music will swell and the cameras will pan up to the sky in a tacit acknowledgement of God's role in bringing you your happy ending.

But what we need to learn—what Isaiah learned and what Paul learned and what all the heroes of the faith learned— is that we are not the main character: God is. It's all about *his* happy ending. He loves you, and he has wonderful plans for you, but they may not be the same plans in the same way at the same time as you had hoped.

Elisabeth Elliot, whose missionary husband was killed by the indigenous people group he was reaching out to in Ecuador in the 1950s, later told of letters she received from people seeking her help and advice—a couple yearning for a child, a young woman who described sitting in "torture and dismay" at her lack of a husband. Elliot wrote in response:

> Our true happiness is to be realized precisely through [God's] refusals, which are always mercies. His choice is flawlessly contrived to give the deepest kind of joy as soon as it is embraced ... Maybe this year will be the year of desire fulfilled. Perhaps, on the other hand, it

will be the year of desire radically transformed, the year of finding, as we have perhaps not truly found, Christ to be the All-Sufficient One, Christ the "deep, sweet well of Love." (*Keep a Quiet Heart*, p 49)

That is my hope and my prayer for you as you continue to pursue the secret of contentment when things haven't turned out as you'd hoped and planned. The road may yet be long, but perhaps this will be for you the year of "If onlys" laid down, desires transformed and Christ discovered in a new way—so that you can say with Paul:

I know what it is to be in need, and I know what it is to have plenty. I have learned the secret of being content in any and every situation, whether well fed or hungry, whether living in plenty or in want. I can do all this through him who gives me strength. (Philippians 4 v 12-13)

You're not alone. God never asks us to do something that he doesn't equip, strengthen and help us to do. The secret is him.

BOOKS REFERENCED

Sam Allberry, *7 Myths About Singleness* (Crossway, 2019)

Alistair Begg, *Pray Big* (The Good Book Company, 2019)

Jeremiah Burroughs, *The Rare Jewel of Christian Contentment* (The Banner of Truth Trust, 1979)

Elisabeth Elliot, *Keep a Quiet Heart* (OM Publishing, 1999)

Rachel Gilson, *Born Again This Way* (The Good Book Company, 2020)

Barbara Johnson, *Splashes of Joy in the Cesspools of Life* (Thomas Nelson, 1992)

Martyn Lloyd-Jones, *Spiritual Depression* (Eerdmans, 1965)

Tanya Marlow, *Those Who Wait* (Malcolm Down Publishing, 2017)

Corrie ten Boom, *The Hiding Place* (Hodder and Stoughton, 1973)

Sheridan Voysey, *Resurrection Year* (Thomas Nelson, 2013)

Rachel and Andrew Wilson, *The Life You Never Expected* (Inter-Varsity Press, 2015)

ACKNOWLEDGEMENTS

I can't begin to name all the people who have loved me, helped me, advocated for me and opened doors for me. They have been generous with their time, encouragements and platforms, and I am incredibly grateful.

When it comes to writing, both technique and opportunity owe much to Nick Spencer, Matthew Hosier and Andrew Wilson. This book was improved by the kind and courageous critique of Sheridan Voysey and the detailed feedback of Jeremy Moses.

Grateful thanks to The Good Book Company team especially Tim Thornborough, Rachel Jones, Joe Henegan and André Parker; Judith Barnett, the keeper of the words; Ali Grafham for faithful prayer; Peter Pollock for songs, laughter and generous encouragement; my Life Group, church leaders and Salt team for their support and input; and of course, my parents. Thanks, Mum and Dad, for introducing me to Jesus so early in life, for always modelling joyful, contented faith in him, and for your unwavering support, encouragement and wisdom.

My cup runneth over.

the good book

C O M P A N Y

BIBLICAL | RELEVANT | ACCESSIBLE

At The Good Book Company, we are dedicated to helping Christians and local churches grow. We believe that God's growth process always starts with hearing clearly what he has said to us through his timeless word—the Bible.

Ever since we opened our doors in 1991, we have been striving to produce Bible-based resources that bring glory to God. We have grown to become an international provider of user-friendly resources to the Christian community, with believers of all backgrounds and denominations using our books, Bible studies, devotionals, evangelistic resources, and DVD-based courses.

We want to equip ordinary Christians to live for Christ day by day, and churches to grow in their knowledge of God, their love for one another, and the effectiveness of their outreach.

Call us for a discussion of your needs or visit one of our local websites for more information on the resources and services we provide.

Your friends at The Good Book Company

thegoodbook.com | thegoodbook.co.uk
thegoodbook.com.au | thegoodbook.co.nz
thegoodbook.co.in